* * *

Saved by
the
Angels

* * *

* * *

Saved by
the
Angels

* * *

*True stories of angels
and near-death experiences*

Glennyce S. Eckersley

RIDER

LONDON • SYDNEY • AUCKLAND • JOHANNESBURG

1 3 5 7 9 10 8 6 4 2

First published in 2002 by Rider,
an imprint of Ebury Press, Random House,
20 Vauxhall Bridge Road, London SW1V 2SA

Random House Australia (Pty) Limited
20 Alfred Street, Milsons Point, Sydney,
New South Wales 2061, Australia

Random House New Zealand Limited
18 Poland Road, Glenfield,
Auckland 10, New Zealand

Random House South Africa (Pty) Limited
Endulini, 5A Jubilee Road,
Parktown 2193, South Africa

The Random House Group Limited Reg. No. 954009

Papers used by Rider are natural, recyclable products made from wood grown in
sustainable forests.

Typeset by MATS, Southend-on-Sea, Essex
Printed and bound by Bookmarque Ltd, Croydon, Surrey

A CIP catalogue record for this book
is available from the British Library

ISBN 0-7126-1217-3

To Valerie Bagarozzi and Yvonne Preston,
with love and gratitude for a lifetime of friendship

'I believe that dreams are more powerful than facts,
That hope always triumphs over experience,
That laughter is the only cure for grief,
And I believe that love is stronger than death.'

ROBERT FULGHUM

∗ ∗ ✳ ∗ ∗

Contents

* * * * *

Preface

Since the days when man first inhabited this world, he has been preoccupied with the next. The belief systems of ancient peoples prominently feature their concept of what the afterlife involves. Hieroglyphics in ancient Egypt, the writings of Zoroaster and the Tibetan Book of the Dead all feature accounts of angels, near-death experiences and death-related visions. The twentieth century saw many volumes produced on these subjects. Historically, science had steadfastly maintained that visions of angels and near-death experiences were mainly figments of the imagination or chemically induced. Serious scientific minds, however, like those of Dr Elisabeth Kübler-Ross and Dr Raymond Moody, have published unbiased studies. Today Dr Moody's book *Life After Life* is twenty-five years old and still a bestseller, so great has been the interest. Dr Peter Fenwick, a consultant neuro-psychiatrist, says 'Consciousness is a fundamental property of the universe, it exists whether we are alive or not. To deny it is to cut out the most important chunk of our experience.' These studies and books have given people 'permission' to talk openly about their experiences and they are doing so in ever increasing numbers.

There has been a phenomenal outpouring of spiritual stories, and the ensuing interest has grown and spread into films, art and music worldwide. Angel encounters have followed on the heels of near-death and out-of-body experiences. No longer are people afraid to reveal their stories, and the sheer numbers of people doing so is proof enough that ordinary mortals are encountering these events in their daily lives. Today the involvement in all spiritually orientated interests is huge. Reiki, for example, or tapping into 'universal life energy', has a philosophical and spiritual basis. Yoga and the Metamorphic Technique (a process similar to reflexology) also work with life forces and energies. Aromatherapy with its wonderful fragrances and mystical air attracts many followers. I have met therapists who tell me they feel angelically guided to the oils suitable for the individual client. Even the popularity of candles with their sacred connotations is evocative of the spiritual and of rituals long rejected. Interestingly, candles are frequently placed amongst flowers, stones and pine cones, forming a personal home altar.

Our times are characterised by a yearning for spirituality. Congregations of religious organisations are running from conventional worship, as quickly as grains of sand from an hourglass. This produces spiritual 'dropouts' who nevertheless feel keenly the resulting vacuum. We are spiritual beings and we long for our spiritual reservoirs to be replenished. We need to make the journey into inner space. There is a strong desire to be reassured that we are not alone, and that a higher source, whatever we may label it, exists. Angel encounters are filling this spiritual gap, confirming that we are cared for, and bringing the message of love so badly needed. We are comforted by their presence, be it perceived as sight, touch, fragrance or voice. In times of danger many people have received help or guidance, or have been rescued. This book is full of true, uplifting stories, from people in every walk of life. In myriad ways, they have been saved by the angels.

* * ✳ * *

Acknowledgements

I am once more indebted to my friend and colleague, David Lomax, for his advice and generous use of resources. A huge thank you to my editor, Judith Kendra, whose cheerful encouragement keeps me on track and makes the whole process such a pleasure. Thanks also to the Principal and staff of New Church College and to Emma Heathcote-James for her friendship. For my friend Greta Woolf, a special thank you for all her support and for Janice O'Gara who cheers me on all the way from Arizona. To Maggie Henderson and Claire Rothwell, thank you for your kindness and cooperation. Special thanks to my daughters, Gillian and Rachel, whose moral and practical support is much appreciated. To my husband, Ross, thank you for keeping your head below the parapet!

Finally, a huge thank you to the very special people who generously allowed me to include their personal stories in this book. They are: George Atherton, Philip Banyard, David Barber, Betty Barnes, Linda Bell, Bloynan, Stephen Bryce, Mary Bullough, Brian Carter, Charles Chizea, Rachel Clark, Hilda Crossley, Margaret Cotton, Christine Dean, Carol Dickson, David and Anne Gaffney, Corrine

Garstang, James Giles, Rosemary Graham, Josie Grimshaw, Heather Greenhalgh, Margaret Hanley, Marion Harding, Irene Hartley, Harry Heap, Sally Hodgeson, Faye Hodson, Ann Hughes, Colin Jacklin, Evengeline Jancey, Marian Kidd, Maya Liamzon, Rod Lewis, Sylvia McDermott, Ruth McDonnell, Janet Morell, Alison Morozzi, Valerie Mulcare-Tivey, Kathryn Murphy, Janice O'Gara, John O'Gara, Pauline O'Gara, Gail Parkinson, Caroline Plant, Catherine Platt, Barbara Price, William Roache, MBE, Gillian Russell, Irena Sadykhova, John Shaw, John Sutcliffe, Stella Thompson, Tony, Andrew Travis, John Walker, Anita Walter, Rochelle Watkins, Roy Wells, Judith White, Deborah Anne Williams and Mark Woolmer. I would also like to thank Audrey, Grace, Jessie, Justine and Sheila.

✳ ✳ ✳ 1 ✳ ✳ ✳

Saved by the Angels

'Did the star-wheels and angel wings, with their holy winnowings
Keep beside you all the way.'
ROBERT BROWNING

By 8 am it was already hot, the day was clearly going to be a scorcher. This was the summer of 1999 and the location was the seaside town of Brighton, England. The town woke to deep blue skies without a cloud to be seen on that beautiful June morning. Roy found the idea of a bike ride irresistible and he took his mountain bike out of the garage for a spin along the seafront. The special bike lane steered him fairly swiftly to the seafront, but by the time of his arrival at the sea, traffic was building in this busy holiday destination. He arrived at the start of the promenade where the special lane terminated and Roy saw to his dismay that he would be forced to join the heavy traffic. Feeling a little vulnerable, he ventured out, conscious of the heavy lorry about to pass him. The lorry travelling on Roy's right-hand side suddenly decided to turn left and, without indicating or even seeing any hazards in his way, the driver cut in front of Roy.

With a sickening thud the lorry hit Roy, rolled over his bike and in so doing dragged Roy underneath! Astonishingly, the driver was apparently unaware of this event and it was only pedestrians and other drivers yelling to him that made him stop. Roy was in a very precarious position indeed. His face was pressed up against one of the giant wheels and his jaw was obviously broken. He could feel the blood flowing into his mouth and the thought went through his head, 'Am I going to die?' It was then that he heard a voice speaking to him in a calming but insistent way. 'Turn your head,' the voice said firmly. In a daze Roy did as he was told with the result that the second heavy wheel passed to the left of his head, narrowly avoiding it. The lorry did roll over Roy's arm and he thought at that point how badly broken it must be. However, the thought that the wheel had only narrowly avoided his head and that that would surely have killed him was a little comfort.

Passers-by were shouting and there was considerable confusion and panic. At this point Roy realised that his sight had gone and this awful realisation added to his fears. Police and firemen arrived on the scene and tried to free him as the ambulance crew waited to help him. Terrified, Roy heard the policeman say that his leg was trapped inside the engine and maybe his back was broken. Dreadful thoughts of paralysis rushed through Roy's mind, and that, he felt, was the only outcome if he survived. Cutting equipment was employed and Roy became aware of an incredible pain starting in his leg. It was as if he was experiencing a nightmare. The voice again spoke to Roy, telling him that all would be well and that he would not die. A cool comforting hand held his gently and a feeling of calm engulfed him. It was a female voice and he concluded that maybe a member of the ambulance crew had somehow managed to crawl under the lorry to help him.

At last he was free from the tangled metal, and as he was lifted clear, his sight mercifully returned. Taking in the scene, he recalls that there was no one under the lorry with him, and no female present, either in the ambulance crew or indeed any of the rescue teams. Decidedly puzzled but greatly relieved he sank into the stretcher and was lifted inside the ambulance to be sped to hospital. Once more the gentle voice whispered in his ear, reassuring him that all would be well. Roy could only ponder on what manner of voice this was and what awaited him at the hospital. To everyone's amazement the appalling injuries that were expected did not in fact present themselves. The leg and foot, so dreadfully trapped, were only badly bruised. The arm over which the enormously heavy lorry had rolled was not broken, again only sustaining bruises. Roy had in fact broken his jaw, but so cleanly and almost exactly in half, which made the repair an easy procedure. It was a miracle in itself that not a single tooth was lost. There have been no serious residual effects from that dreadful accident. Medical staff, relatives and friends were confused and perplexed as to how this could possibly be.

What about Roy? What are his thoughts and feelings of that day? He now has no doubt about the source of that calming voice. 'It was,' he says, 'my guardian angel making the whole ordeal as painless and injury-free as possible.' As Roy said to me when concluding his incredible story: 'I thank my guardian angel each night for the gift of life but also for the amazing gift of love.'

Our next story comes from the southern states of the USA. A world away in many senses from Brighton, but the need of an angel was just as great. Here is what happened on a June day in Phoenix, Arizona.

It was a beautiful day. The heat was dry and the sky azure blue. Driving home from a shopping trip, Janice thought how lucky she was to be living in such a lovely place. Resident in the state for only two years, she and her husband nevertheless felt very much at home. Wide open spaces and vast skyscapes enthralled them, not to mention the wonderful colours of the rocks and desert sunsets. It was all so different from the England they had left behind. It was 5 pm and the traffic was building as Janice drove homeward, keeping to the speed limit of forty-five mph. Approaching traffic lights on green, Janice, on the inside lane, intended to drive straight ahead and so she continued through the lights.

At this point she was horrified to see a car cutting immediately in front of her vehicle. She went cold with fear, realising that she did not have any chance of avoiding it. The impact made a deafening sound as Janice hit the car, buckling into the mercifully empty passenger seat. On impact the airbag of Janice's car deployed and then exploded and she was engulfed in a white snowstorm of chemicals. This was the last thing she could remember for some time, and the events that followed are a mystery to her. Regaining consciousness, Janice found herself still inside the car but not in the middle of the road. She was gently coming to a halt in a side road well out of harm's way, where no further cars would be involved.

Disorientated, she was aware of people trying to help her and extract her from the car. How on earth she had arrived in a place of safety in the side road she had no idea. Firstly the car was a write-off and theoretically should not have been capable of moving after the impact. How it had extracted itself from the position it had been in, namely firmly embedded in the other vehicle, was another mystery. A witness said the car had slowly reversed from the tangled metal and gently steered itself into the side road, thus avoiding what might have been a multiple pile-up. Janice says she lost conciousness as soon as the airbag exploded and that there was no way she had driven that car. Her main injuries were burns from the chemicals in the airbag affecting her arms and face. She would not have been able to see in any event, due to the chemical snowstorm, which completely filled the car interior making visibility zero.

Members of the rescue services were totally puzzled, not least as to how a car so badly damaged had moved even an inch, let alone steered itself into a side road! Arriving at the hospital, Janice learned that the driver of the other car, although having to be cut from his vehicle, was completely unhurt. That in itself was declared to be a minor miracle by all concerned. No broken bones were discovered or internal injuries revealed, which proved to be yet another puzzle to the medical team. No one seemed to have an explanation for this extraodinary event. However, Janice has no doubt in her mind about just what happened that evening; she states categorically that she was 'saved by the angels'.

Dachshunds, it seems to me, have been physically shortchanged, especially in the leg department. Mitzi, however, was one very sweet little dog who had reason to be glad of her diminutive height and the ease with which she could be carried one night. Her owner, Judith, had moved into her parents' bungalow for a time and was looking after things whilst they were on holiday. She pondered on the fact that there were many advantages to be had in owning a bungalow instead of a house, maintenance being an obvious one. The bungalow's temperamental boiler, however, did not seem to be an advantage even though it was easily accessible. It was quite a struggle to come to terms with this monster. A list of instructions had been left for Judith and special details of the boiler were included. This said boiler was of the solid fuel variety and required 'banking up' each evening with coal to ensure a constant supply of hot water. The technique required was a little delicate, and if not performed correctly, the thing would go out. However, assuring them all would be well in their absence, she had waved her parents off cheerfully. It was a lovely peaceful evening as she and Mitzi settled down for their evening meal. Bedtime came and Judith triumphed with the boiler technique and there were lashings of hot water for her bath.

Morning number three dawned and to Judith's dismay the water was stone-cold. She groaned, knowing only too well that the task of relighting the monster would not be an easy one. Battle with the boiler commenced and on the following night Judith decided that perhaps there had not been enough coal stoked into the iron maiden to keep it alight. She shovelled more coal onto the pile and went to bed fervently hoping the water would be hot when she woke. One thing Judith was jolly good at was sleeping – she was capable of falling asleep as soon as her head touched the pillow and almost never woke before morning. This particular night was no exception and she fell into a sound sleep almost immediately. In the middle of the night Judith was awakened by a very loud man's voice shouting her name and urging her to wake up. Normally Judith would sleep through a loud alarm clock, and getting little response the voice became louder and more insistent. 'The boiler is overheating,' the voice warned, 'you must get out of bed.' Leaping out of bed, Judith knew this was not a dream but she was unable to trace where the voice was coming from. There was no one in her bedroom and a search of the bungalow revealed no one.

Entering the kitchen Judith found Mitzi shaking in fright in the middle of the floor; the boiler was making frightful noises. Glancing at the temperature gauge Judith saw the dial was at nought, and, perplexed, she thought at first this indicated that the boiler had gone out. The noises, however, became louder and were unlike any she had heard before. Opening the boiler door she was horrified to see huge flames and she realised even in her sleepy, confused state that the fact the dial had registered nought did not in fact mean that the boiler had gone out. Quite the contrary, the dial indicated that it had travelled all the way around, indicating serious overheating.

Transfixed with fear for a moment, Judith had no idea what to do next but was suddenly galvanised into action as the pipes started banging and shaking. Scooping up the tiny dog and tucking it under her arm she fled the building. Running down the lane she reached the nearest neighbour's house and banged on the door. She chuckles in retrospect at the sight she must have presented to the startled man as he opened the door in the middle of the night. White with fright and in her nightdress and barefoot, she stood shaking with the dog under her arm! 'I must have looked like Dorothy from the Wizard of Oz,' she says.

The kind man mercifully soon grasped the situation, and knew exactly what had to be done. Rushing back to the bungalow he turned all the taps on full to relieve the pressure and eventually his ministrations calmed the boiler and rendered it safe. It had been a night to remember and the terrified Judith was extremely grateful to the neighbour. The parents returned and Judith and the neighbour related the story to the stunned pair. They were all startled when the neighbour said, 'Did the dog bark and warn you? If you had not woken when you did, the whole thing would have exploded, with consequences that do not bear thinking about.' Knowing how soundly her daughter slept,

Judith's mother asked what had managed to wake her. She told her mother about the voice and how insistent it had been, ensuring she got out of bed. Smiling knowingly, Judith's mother said in a very matter-of-fact way, 'It must have been your guardian angel.' Judith truly believes to this day that it really was.

> *'Hush! my dear, lie still and slumber,*
> *Holy angels guard thy bed*
> *Heavenly blessings without number*
> *Gently falling on thy head.'*
> ISAAC WATTS

Any woman who has been pregnant will tell you what an emotional roller-coaster the condition can be. The overriding concern, however, is always for the safety and protection of the tiny life growing inside. Gail was at the point in her pregnancy where the news was really just sinking in and it did feel like a huge responsibility.

One night when she had been fast asleep, she suddenly awakened for no apparent reason. She sat up in bed, wide awake and decidedly confused. There had been no sudden noise to disturb her and she felt perfectly well. It was as if one minute she was deeply asleep and the next sitting bolt upright. It was a very odd feeling. To her astonishment, straight ahead of her in the darkness she saw a figure emerging at the foot of the bed. The figure was slowly surrounded by bright light growing in intensity and a golden outer glow emerged, radiating outwards from the figure. The initial feeling was one of alarm. The figure was, she thought, definitely contacting her because it had appeared on her side of the bed. It seemed to Gail that this figure was male in gender. She glanced at her husband who was soundly sleeping, and considered waking him.

But finding she was incapable of moving, she gazed in awe at the figure, her fear gradually subsiding. No words were spoken or gestures made, but somehow Gail understood that this was a message concerning her unborn child. Instinctively she placed her hands protectively across her stomach.

Much to Gail's surprise, as the figure vanished, she lay down and fell instantly into a deep sleep. On waking there was a great deal of confusion in Gail's mind as to what it could have meant. She even thought she might have imagined it all or should dismiss it as a dream. It all seemed so improbable that she decided to keep the incident private and tell no one. In due course Joe was born a healthy, happy baby, to everyone's relief. He was greatly loved and the family felt truly blessed.

When Joe was fifteen months old, Gail took him upstairs in the house one day, placing him to play in the bedroom. Downstairs the carpets were being cleaned professionally and the little boy had to be amused away from this operation. Gail decided to catch up on her ironing in the next bedroom because Joe appeared to be contentedly playing with his many toys. An almighty crash startled Gail, who immediately ran white-faced into the next bedroom. The sight that met her turned her legs to jelly. A huge, heavy wooden wardrobe had fallen on top of Joe. Realising that her little boy was underneath this enormous piece of furniture made Gail scream in terror. Quite apart from anything else, there was no way Gail could lift this heavy object. Her screaming brought the man cleaning the carpets rushing from the room below. His face too turned ashen on absorbing the situation. Gingerly they lifted the wardrobe, fearful of what they might find.

Joe crawled from underneath, asking where his teddy was! The wardrobe door had apparently swung open, enabling the little boy to be trapped in the hollow inside. He did not suffer even a scratch. Gail leapt forward, scooping him up in her arms and shaking with emotion. Scratching his head in bewilderment the carpet cleaner exclaimed, 'Good God, Gail, someone up there likes you!' Yes, thought Gail, perplexed.

Time passed and Joe was three years old when one cold, bright December day Gail decided to take him to see Father Christmas. He will just be the right age to understand the concept, she thought, and it would be fun for her also. The weather was lovely, seasonally crisp and sunny with deep blue skies. Gail decided that they would walk to one of the large town stores. Reaching the busy main road they stopped at the traffic lights. Without warning and with sickening speed, Joe pulled his hand away from Gail's and ran into the middle of the busy road.

In the centre of this road was a traffic island and all Gail could do was pray that he would reach it safely. All would be well if he would stay there until she could get to him. No such luck. Joe carried on running unsteadily as a large car swooped down on him with no obvious way of avoiding the little figure. Gail thought her heart would stop as she gazed helplessly at this dreadful scene. The most amazing thing happened next: Joe, who had been running forwards, suddenly sat down hard on his bottom. His legs buckled underneath him as if something had simply swept them from the floor. He sat statue-like as the huge car drove past at speed, missing him by a whisker. It occurred to Gail later that had Joe fallen forwards it would have been disastrous – after all, that is the way children usually fall when running fast, she mused. Rushing to pick him up, Gail with wobbly legs carried him safely to the opposite side of the road. A pedestrian shook his head in amazement, declaring to Gail that what he had just witnessed was hard to believe.

This second incident made Gail think again about the night she had seen the figure at the foot of her bed. She knew without doubt now that it had been an angel visitation. Her feelings at the time that the visit must be connected with the unborn baby seemed to be correct. 'This could only have been a guardian angel,' Gail says. She realises others may choose to disbelieve her, but having witnessed these incidents, she knows deep inside she has arrived at the right conclusion.

It is a fact of life that for most of us to reach a location of peace and natural beauty, we must first travel through heavy traffic and on busy motorways. Even worse is the fact that after spending some time in such peaceful havens we then have to face the homeward journey. After feeling so close to nature the reality of noise and traffic seem surreal.

This was exactly how Pauline was feeling after several days on retreat in the blissful surroundings of the Lake District. Her spiritual journey was now swiftly followed by the everyday reality of the M60 motorway. For some time Pauline had been mulling over the idea of abandoning her career and pursuing a more spiritual path. A teacher of yoga and Reiki, she felt drawn to these pursuits on a full-time basis. There were of course financial implications with such a move and it was not an easy decision.

Arriving at the motorway slip road, Pauline found her thoughts turning to this dilemma once more and the pull to follow her heart seemed stronger than ever. Joining the motorway she drove at a steady pace on the inside lane – it was not terrifically busy but traffic was gradually building. Without warning there was a sickening crashing noise as a car ploughed into the back of Pauline's. Propelled forwards in the vehicle she found to her panic that her foot had jammed on the accelerator pedal. She was hurtling out of control across all the lanes of the motorway, narrowly avoiding traffic by the second. With mounting panic she tried to control this weaving across the lanes. Miraculously she eventually reached the safety of the hard shoulder. How she had avoided a collision she could not imagine and she felt as if an unseen hand had driven the car. Finally, releasing her foot from the pedal, she managed to come to a full stop, shaking and wobbly from the experience. With utter astonishment she heard a loud voice proclaim, 'Kick up the backside!' Turning round, Pauline could see no one anywhere near, and there was certainly only herself in the car. Amazingly, there was no sign of the car that had hit her from behind and to say that she was confused is an under-statement.

Aware at this point of a pain in her neck – clearly whiplash – she thought it seemed advisable to make her way home gingerly and with great care. It did appear to have been a lucky escape, all things considered, and it was hard to believe a whiplash injury was the only problem she had. Eventually she arrived home and, after thankfully sinking into an armchair, she rang the police. Despite intensive investigations and enquiries, the police could find no trace of the accident. There was no sign of the other car involved despite the obvious evidence of the severely crushed rear end of Pauline's car. It was quite a mystery. Over the course of the next few days the accident took on a symbolic meaning for Pauline. Coupled with the voice it all seemed to indicate that a change of life was called for. I must, she thought, cease dashing around in all directions and follow my heart towards a more peaceful path.

Reaching this all-important decision, Pauline resigned from her professional position and took a leap of faith. It has proved to be exactly the right decision. The demand for her teaching, workshops and weekend retreats has mushroomed to meet an ever-increasing need. A spiritual gap is being filled and Pauline feels great satisfaction. How very apt, she says, was that kick up the backside!

Our next rescue story is very different in nature from Pauline's. The angel who rescued David was very familiar indeed.

At the age of thirty-eight David was a busy working nurse. Extremely practical and intelligent, he enjoyed his job and his happy family life. His young son was especially fond of swimming, and one day it was decided that David and his wife would take him to the local pool to watch him swim. They were both proud of the fact that he was a strong swimmer, especially as neither David nor his wife could actually swim. Arriving at the pool, David felt a longing to go into the water and whilst his wife sat by the pool reading her magazine he slipped in to join his son. Bobbing along, he approached the deeper end of the pool, which was six feet in depth. David moved forward, reasoning that he was five feet ten inches and therefore could not possibly be in danger – after all, a little jump of only a few inches would keep him on the surface.

Unfamiliar with swimming pools or how the water affects us he was totally unprepared when his foot slipped and he fell to the bottom of the tiled pool. The shock of finding himself lying on the tiles at the bottom brought on panic and he thrashed about, unable to rise to the surface. Opening his mouth in this awful panic, he felt the searing pain of water entering his lungs. He describes the pain as a sensation of molten lava being poured into him. Oddly, he could see his wife sitting by the pool unaware of the drama below the surface. The thought entered David's head that no one realised he was in such trouble and he resigned himself to the fact that he was actually going to die and this would be his last moment. Drowning, he concluded, was not only frightening but amazingly swift.

He also at this point saw the figure of his son swimming happily lower down the pool. This is the last thing I shall ever see, he thought. It was then that he saw, underneath the figure of his son, a strange mist forming, coming through the water towards him. The pain in his lungs was by now excruciating, but from the mist there emerged a figure. As the figure grew closer he felt the pain subside and he recognised the form of his much loved grandmother. She was clothed in a long white gown with her hair streaming in the water behind her and David stared transfixed. He had loved her very much, but knew that she had been dead for many years. The pain had by now completely gone and David was aware of arms slipping underneath him and a gentle lifting movement. There was another sensation simultaneously and that was of his son trying also to lift him. His son had become aware of David's predicament and was trying to lift him by his hair. The boy was very slight, whereas David is substantially built. Clearly, his young son would never have been able to lift such a dead weight from the pool bottom.

David lost consciousness and the next thing he can remember is lying on the side of the pool with attendants working on him to remove the water from his lungs. He had survived against the odds, having been underwater and in trouble for some considerable time. His memory of the event is extremely lucid and he has no doubt whatsoever that his guardian angel saved him that day and amazingly it was his grandmother. He can feel the overwhelming sensations of love to this day. He says the most lasting impression, however, is that, come what may, he will never be afraid to die. He is convinced that we have a wonderful life waiting in the world beyond and that the angel of death is really a loved one waiting to greet us in the next world.

Our next story concerns an angelic rescue, no doubt about it, but in a very unusual way. Colin was a taxi driver and after a long, busy evening dropped his last two customers safely home and decided to call it a night. It was 2.30 am and he was anxious to reach home. Driving down the main road that would bring him to his own front door, he longed for a cup of tea and the warmth of his own fire. Without warning, the steering wheel guided the car sharply to the left. Colin tried to turn the wheel back on course but it simply would not budge. He did the only thing possible under the circumstances and applied his brakes sharply. Stopping with a jolt he found himself facing the correct way in a one-way street. Climbing from his car, he inspected the front wheels but could find nothing untoward. On entering the car once more, he found that the steering wheel now appeared to be functioning correctly. Puzzled, he drove off, but very slowly and with great caution.

Approximately halfway down this very dark side street, Colin saw something in his headlights. An unidentifiable black heap lay in the middle of the road. Drawing slowly closer, Colin saw that it was the prone figure of a policeman. Leaping from the car, Colin checked the man's vital signs; clearly he was unconscious. With as much haste as care would allow, he placed him on the back seat of his car and rushed him to hospital. Pulling up at the entrance of the accident and emergency unit, he saw two policemen outside and they quickly took over as Colin related the event to them. Feeling that he done all he could and knowing that the policeman was now in safe hands, he headed for home once more.

At last he entered his own street and stopped outside his home. It was then that the most remarkable event of the evening took place. A large, bright light appeared in front of the car; it was in no way so bright as to be blinding, but soft and glowing. As he gazed at this wonderful light, there slowly emerged in its very centre a face. The face was smiling and so very gentle, exuding calmness and pure happiness. Colin felt all these emotions sweep over him and he thought to himself that this must be the most extra-ordinary night of his life.

The following evening a police inspector accompanied by two patrol officers arrived at Colin's house. They had traced him through the taxi office and wished to tell him that he had saved the policeman's life. He was invited to go into the police station for official thanks, but Colin declined. 'How could I accept the credit,' he says, 'when it was in fact the angel that saved the man's life. It was the angel that turned the wheel of the car and directed me to the spot where he lay.' And then with a twinkle, he added, 'Can you imagine trying to explain that to a room full of policemen?'

'What angel nightly tracks that waste of frozen snow.'
EMILY BRONTË

Stories of angel rescue can be very dramatic, as you have read, but none more so than Marion's amazing account. Her story begins many years ago, but the details of this particular night are crystal-clear in her mind.

It was a bitterly cold winter night; icicles hung from every windowsill and roof. It was treacherous underfoot, the ice having been covered by a heavy fall of snow. Walking slowly and with great care, Marion and her boyfriend were making their way to her boyfriend's home. They were looking forward to the warmth of a glowing fire and the hot meal that awaited them. Christmas had just passed and Marion, nineteen years old at the time, was chatting excitedly about the events of the holiday. The streets were deserted, everyone was indoors away from the cold, and no cars ventured onto the roads in such severe conditions. They passed the bleak-looking train station and approached the path they needed to take to reach the house.

Without warning, Marion shouted loudly that they must stop, insisting that they could not continue down that particular road. 'Why ever not?' her boyfriend asked. Her answer was more startling than her yell. 'Can't you see the angel,' was the reply, 'warning us not to go that way?' Her boyfriend could see nothing and chided her for being fanciful. Marion insisted, however, that the angel was real and very large. Traditional in appearance, it had huge white wings stretching from above its head to the ground. Clothed in a long white gown, it was surrounded by a bright glow. It was clear to Marion that this was a warning and that the angel was there specifically to protect them. She had a sensation that the angel was male and heeded his warning by insisting that they did not move any further down their intended path.

Almost instantly a loud noise filled the clear cold night, deafening in intensity. With incredulity they watched as a huge telegraph pole snapped in two, crashing to the ground immediately in front of them. The heavy pole and all the live wires hit the snow and ice, spectacularly bursting into flames. This was of course on the very spot where they would have then been had the angel not warned them. Marion's boyfriend was speechless. Marion has no doubt in her mind whatsoever about what she saw and indeed why she saw it. Unquestionably, that night they had been saved by the angel.

Rescue from above takes many forms; not all are dramatic, life-saving situations but are instead gentle and timely. To the person concerned they are being rescued nevertheless, and the intervention comes as a huge relief. This was certainly true for Betty. One day she received a phone call from her cousin, who was planning a holiday and wished Betty to accompany her. 'I know your first instinct is to say no,' Betty's cousin remarked, 'but do think about it carefully.' A huge sigh came from Betty's very heart. 'I will take the plunge and come with you to America,' she said. It had been a difficult year for Betty; making even the smallest decision was a burden, never mind a large, important one like travelling across the Atlantic. Just twelve months previously, with dreadful suddenness, her much loved husband Peter had died. It had been a terrific shock and one she thought at the time she would never recover from. A wonderful husband, kind and caring and very protective, Peter had been someone with whom Betty always felt safe and secure. Here she was being persuaded to take a holiday without him for the first time in her life. How, she wondered, would she ever cope? Her cousin told her that a change of scenery and a new country would be a valuable tonic, and she booked the holiday swiftly before Betty could change her mind. It seemed to Betty that she would scarcely have the energy or the will to complete this trip, but she decided to try; her cousin after all had her best interests at heart.

Betty's children were very supportive and her friends endorsed her decision with their encouragement and so she set forth on the big adventure. She told herself that Peter would have wished it and for his sake she would be brave. Boston was to be their destination and before long the departure day arrived. All went smoothly and soon they were wandering around the city of Boston, taking in the sights and history of the place. England did feel a long way away to Betty and the whole trip had a rather unreal air about it. She felt rather detached at times as she tried hard to enjoy everything. One day they decided to go into the city for a shopping expedition. Lots of gifts to buy for the family back home and perhaps a few treats for herself, Betty thought. The day proved to be very successful, if a little tiring, and it was with relief that Betty sank on to the platform seat and waited for the train to take them back to their hotel. Parcels at her feet, she was thinking what a welcome sight the train would be. Her head ached a little and her feet ached a great deal, and so it was with thankful hearts that they climbed aboard the train and settled into the comfortable seats. Arranging their purchases on the seats beside them they cheerfully said that they would soon be back at the hotel for a hot bath and a meal.

Fear suddenly rushed through Betty's veins as she realised to her horror that although she had picked up her many shopping bags she had left her handbag on the platform seat. This was nothing short of a disaster, for it contained everything valuable and essential. There were her travellers' cheques and cash, several credit cards and even her passport. What on earth could she do? This was her worst nightmare. Sheer dismay overcame Betty and they decided the only thing to do was to alight at the next staion and consider their options. The pair hurried from the train at the next stop and, seeing an official, explained their predicament. Betty asked if he would telephone the previous station to enquire if the bag had been handed in. The official roared with laughter. 'Lady,' he replied, 'this is America,' and added that never in all his considerable working life as a railway official had he ever heard of an important piece of luggage being handed in.

Seeing the despair on Betty's face he agreed to try. He went into his little office on the platform and the two waited, feeling very low indeed. A few minutes later the man emerged from the office, a look of incredulity on his face. The bag, he announced, had indeed been handed in and would be returned to her forthwith. Everyone was totally amazed except Betty. 'Someone up there is taking care of you lady,' said the man. 'Yes,' replied Betty, 'it is Peter.'

Symbols in nature can be very powerful. Take the tree, for instance; it is not only a source of inspiration and beauty but has great symbolic meaning. The very fact that its roots are deep and firmly anchored whilst it branches reach up seemingly to heaven is strong imagery in itself. The delicate tracery of the leaves contrasts sharply with the solidity of the trunk; for sheer beauty it takes some beating. I recall being deeply moved by Dennis Potter's last television interview just prior to his death. He told Melvin Bragg how touched he was by the blossoms outside his bedroom window. He knew it would be his last spring and said they were 'the blossomest blossom' he had ever seen! In spite of everything, he could appreciate the beauty of the trees. In ancient times people believed that trees had their own spirits and would touch a tree to communicate with its spirit and ask for its help. This is the origin of the expression 'touch wood'. If the help was forthcoming the fortunate person would then go and thank the tree, knocking on the trunk in gratitude. This then is the source of the expression 'knock on wood'. Lying under a large leafy tree in summer looking up at a clear blue sky can be a magical experience and soon puts problems into perspective.

*'Stars and blossoming fruit trees: Utter permanence
and extreme fragility give an equal sense of eternity.'*
SIMONE WEIL

Children adore trees – climbing them, or stringing a
hammock between their branches or attaching a swing,
they find them the most wonderful playthings. The most
magical experience of all seems to be when a child owns a
treehouse. Sitting high in the branches in one's own little
house can feel to a child like the nearest thing to heaven.
Certainly our next story indicates that Michael was closer
to heaven than he imagined, for the angels were certainly
very near. Fortunate enough to live in a house with a large
garden and some very solid old trees, Michael had been
built a treehouse as a birthday gift. How he loved it, and
many small items of furniture had been ferried up to add to
his delight. The arrival of the summer holidays saw Michael
and his friends spending most days in the treehouse.

At the end of one gloriously hot summer day, Michael's
friends reluctantly climbed down to head home for their
evening meals. Dirty and happy from their day of
imaginative play, they left Michael sitting alone with just
his cat Holly for company. Several times he heard his
mother call him, but he could not bring himself to leave his
eyrie. At last he slowly started to descend with his beloved
tabby cat under his arm. As they left the treehouse
entrance, however, Holly wriggled free, and Michael lost
his balance. It was a frightening sensation as he catapulted
towards earth.

Walking down the garden with the intention of

extracting her son from his tree, Sarah, Michael's mother, caught her breath as she watched her son fall. Breaking into a run she knew instinctively that she could not reach him before he hit the ground. Who knows what injuries might occur or how badly he might be hurt, she thought. A fraction before the impact, Michael felt strong arms encircle him and place him gently on the ground. He imagined that somehow his father must have caught him. Lying on the grass he saw no one except his mother breathlessly running up to him. Puzzled, the pair stared at each other. 'It is amazing,' his mother said. 'You seemed to stop in mid-air.' Michael sat up, not a scratch or bruise to be seen, and he recalled no sensation of impact with the hard ground at all. It was difficult to believe and as he related he the story to his father he declared that he had no possible explanation. Later that night, Sarah confided to her husband that the only conclusion she could come to was that Michael had been saved by his guardian angel. She expected her husband to rebuke her for being silly but he said with a very hushed tone, 'I really think you are right, and one day Michael will too.'

Michael may learn to believe in angels. However, for one young lady her belief was strong before her need of them arose and it has certainly never wavered since.

It was one of those days that make the most miserable of souls feel cheerful. Deep blue skies, sparkling sunshine bouncing off flowers and trees and making the colours intense. It was the end of a busy working day for Faye and she looked forward to the lovely evening when she could relax outdoors. Cheerily waving goodbye to colleagues she climbed into her car, noting how lovely the blossoms looked and how intense was their fragrance.

She had only driven a little way towards home when she became alarmed at the sight of a car travelling at great speed in the opposite direction and apparently heading straight for her. She only had time to wonder if it was in fact out of control when the impact happened. Unsurprisingly, details of the actual collision are sketchy in Faye's mind. She recalls opening her eyes sometime later to realise that although she had in fact survived the head-on collision, she was trapped in her vehicle. The whole front part of the car was weighing heavily upon her and it was obvious that she would have to be cut free. It felt as though many bones were broken, her arm obviously so, and it was very painful. The emergency services arrived and swiftly realised that it was not going to be an easy task to free Faye although they tried their best to be reassuring. Severe shock was setting in at this point and Faye was shivering with cold. Quickly she was swathed in blankets but even so the cold felt numbing. A very young lady and a fairly new driver, this was a dreadful experience for Faye and she recalls desperately wishing for her mother to be there. The scene was one of chaos and very frightening. Faye was losing a lot of blood from her injuries, making her feel dizzy. The cold intensified and soon she was slipping in and out of consciousness as the paramedics worked feverishly to try and free her. She was urged by every means possible to try to keep her eyes open, but she had been trapped and in pain for a long time now and it was becoming increasingly difficult to be brave.

It was at this point that something amazing occurred: the awful noise of the cutting equipment vanished along with the shouting. She felt instantly warm and at peace, waves of love washing over her, and for the first time since the moment of the accident she felt completely safe. A presence that defied description comforted Faye; she simply knew she was receiving help to get her through and was convinced that this was her guardian angel.

Freed at last, she was swiftly taken to hospital where the full extent of her injuries was revealed. They were indeed very severe and Faye would be in hospital for many weeks to come. However, during the whole of this time, Faye is convinced of the angel's presence, helping her through the considerable trauma. Not only was the recovery from the physical injuries a long and demanding process but the mental and emotional strain was considerable. Faye says that her angel was there for her when she needed her most and without this presence she doubts that she would have pulled through.

Eventually Faye returned to health and strength and the awful events were behind her. She had a powerful feeling that she needed a tangible reminder of her angel's help but was at a loss as to what form this might take. Talking to a good friend, she was delighted when he came up with what she thought was the perfect solution. He designed an angel tattoo for her which she, and indeed everyone else, would see as a permanent memento of a heavenly helper. Maybe one day you will see a lively young lady with a very attractive little angel tattoed on her ankle. You can be pretty sure it is Faye and you will know exactly why it is there.

Here I sit on a cold, grey, rainy day in Manchester, trying to picture life in the Philippines, with all the sun one can possibly want. The islands, bordered as they are by the South China Sea and the mighty Pacific, evoke scenes one can only dream about. Imagine the palms, the fine white beaches and the heat. Maya thought it a most beautiful and comfortable place to live and she enjoyed her life immensely. The family business was real estate and she and her husband had enjoyed great success. They had a very beautiful house and an elegant lifestyle. Maya says the house was filled with wonderful artwork, porcelain and furnishings. They sold houses to the rich and famous and ten years of hard work building the business were paying dividends.

One dreadful night would change this lifestyle for ever; Maya says it all vanished in the twinkling of an eye. In the early hours of the morning, around 1.15 am, Maya was suddenly roused from a deep sleep by the sounds of shouting. Sleepily she wondered where the voices were coming from and then pondered on the fact that they might have burglars downstairs. Slipping out of bed, she then realised that the voices were in fact coming from outside the perimeter fence of the house and warning her of smoke billowing from the building. Running downstairs, Maya entered the kitchen and saw that the generator in the corner of the kitchen was partially in flames and the utility cupboard immediately adjacent was also ablaze. It seemed perfectly logical to Maya, in her sleepy state and in the shock of finding flames in her kitchen, to throw water on it. The fire appeared small enough to be extinguished quickly and she filled a container with water and started to run towards the seat of the fire. Before she could reach the flames, her feet went from under her and she slipped, spilling the water all over the kitchen floor. She tried once more, yet again her feet went from under her and she spilt the water. Three times in all she tried and each time it felt as if someone was deliberately knocking her legs from beneath her.

It was at this point that Maya became aware of shouting from the upper floors; members of her staff were obviously trapped in their quarters. Rushing upstairs she reached the door leading to the staff quarters, only to find it locked from the inside. Screams were obviously coming from the far end of the bedroom and people were trying to escape through the window. This totally confused Maya; why, she wondered, had they not unlocked the door and run down the stairs as she had? Knocking furiously on the door to no avail she decided that there was little she could do and as the smoke was now thick, black and choking she realised that she must save herself.

With relief Maya reached the street and was delighted to see her family and all the staff safely assembled. They in turn were thrilled to see her, convinced as they were that she had perished in the kitchen. Two separate versions of the night now emerged. Maya had been aware of only a small fire in the kitchen, others had seen an inferno. This was confirmed by people who had seen the sequence of events from outside the house. The people trapped in the staff quarters had escaped through the window because, having peeped outside the bedroom door, they had been met by a wall of flames and smoke! It was all very confusing, and the events seemed even more astonishing when they talked to the fire services after the fire had been extinguished. Firstly they told Maya that had she managed to throw water on the flames as she had intended, she would have been instantly electrocuted. It was then pointed out to her that had she managed to open the bedroom door (which was not in fact locked) she would have created a backdraft, producing an inferno from which she could not possibly have escaped.

Reflecting on these facts, Maya shook with fear at what might have been. 'I was it seems in a protective bubble, not realising the ferocity of the fire or the danger I was in,' she said. 'My feet were definitely knocked from under me deliberately and I was prevented from opening the bedroom door.' She realised also that she had run up and down the stairs in only her flimsy nightdress and her bare feet. That the nightdress had not caught fire was in itself a minor miracle. So many questions filled Maya's mind. What had protected her? How had she escaped unharmed down the blazing flight of stairs? It was as if time itself had been frozen to allow her to escape.

Eventually another piece of the puzzle emerged. It had

happened the night before the dreadful fire at about 10 pm. Maya's staff witnessed a strange, bright light outside their window. It stayed for several seconds and they could find no explanation for it. Suddenly everything fell into place for Maya; she feels the light was a warning and all the help she received that night was from her angel. There was simply no other explanation, in her opinion. A good friend of Maya's bought her my book *An Angel at My Shoulder* to console her after the loss of her home. Amazed, she read of all the other people helped in difficult circumstances by angels. The book confirmed for her what she had already assumed: her angel had been there to rescue her on that dreadful night.

Maya now paints and designs angels, having considerable success with her artwork in the USA. She tells me that she knows without doubt that the worst night of her life could in fact have been the last night of her life, had it not been for her angel. She urged me to write her story because she wants as many people as possible to learn of her miraculous escape and to believe in the angels.

From the heat of the Philippines we return once more to winter in England and sympathise with Florence, who had no desire to go outside and face the bitter day.

Pulling on her warm winter boots and topcoat, Florence shivered involuntarily. How she wished that she could stay indoors. Glancing through the window at the sharp frost making a very picturesque scene, she thought it did look beautiful but walking would be decidedly treacherous. There was no alternative, though, she would have to go to the shops – food was running low and Marmalade, her large ginger cat, would wake up hungry any moment. An icy blast of air greeted Florence as she stepped outside, making her ears tingle as she hurried as fast as she could to the corner store. Having enjoyed a little chat with a neighbour or two, it was time to face the elements again and return home.

The pavements were terribly slippy and Florence was grateful that she did not have far to walk. When almost to her door and within sight of her warm little house, she suddenly lost her footing. The ice was pretty thick at that point and with a feeling of panic she felt her two feet slide from under her, realising instantly that a fall at the age of seventy-eight years old would almost certainly result in a bad break. 'Help,' she cried, although how on earth anyone could, she did not know. Unseen hands suddenly caught her seconds before she hit the ground and she then describes how she was lifted to her feet by a spiritual force. She is simply unable to think of another way of describing the action that lifted her once more to safety. Collecting herself, she looked around. There was no one in sight, the street completely was deserted, and yet her shopping bag was upturned, her purchases spilt, proof that she had actually fallen and not just imagined the episode.

Retrieving her shopping she gingerly managed the last few steps to her door and safety. Making a cup of tea to steady her nerves, Florence sank with relief into her comfy armchair. It did not take her long to come to the conclusion that her guardian angel had rescued her. Often in life, she says, she had the feeling that she was being watched over but this was the first time the angels had actually intervened and saved her.

In a word-association questionnaire what image would the following words produce? Holly, gifts, carols, happiness. It could only be Christmas, could it not? Concentrate on the word Christmas and you can almost smell the turkey and hear the family laughter. For many people, however, the reality can be very different. The day may have tragic associations, compounded by the very nature of the day itself. This is certainly the case for Brian, who experienced a Christmas some years ago he will never forget.

Arriving at his mother's house with his wife and two children Brian was looking forward to a happy family day. Hugging and kissing followed by the opening of parcels started the day. The children were delighted and his wife and mother then retired to the kitchen to prepare the traditional family lunch. Brian and his father decided at this point to have a pre-lunch drink. It seemed a very agreeable idea and so they sauntered happily down to the local pub for a short time. A wonderful meal with all the trimmings awaited them on their return and everyone enjoyed a blissful afternoon. Early evening arrived and Brian had the idea that a cousin of his living not too far away might like to join them for the rest of the evening. It was only a few minutes' drive away and the cousin was delighted to be invited. Brian started the car, telling everyone he would be back in a short time.

It had been several hours since Brian had indulged in his lunchtime drink and he felt that driving would be safe. He felt more than capable of the short journey but was dismayed to see how the weather had deteriorated. Heavy rain made visibility difficult and produced almost a haze. Approaching a bend in the road, Brian was taken aback when a large, white car suddenly pulled out in front of him from a car park. Swerving to miss the vehicle he hit a brick wall, and that was the last thing he could remember of that journey. It appeared that what actually happened was that the car plunged straight through the wall, coming to a violent halt at the top of a very steep railway embankment. The force of this sudden halt catapulted Brian through the windscreen and down the steep embankment. He landed heavily at the bottom of the slope, unconscious.

The following sequence of events is quite astonishing but clearly recalled by Brian. He was 'out of his body', sitting at the top of the slope watching himself. He saw his gradual return to consciousness and how he struggled to get to his feet. Continuing to observe, he recalls thinking how badly injured his real self appeared to be. Bizarrely he saw the struggle as the figure heaved itself painfully up the steep embankment. He very matter-of-factly noted how heavily Brian was bleeding, but could feel no pain or distress in his out-of-body state. Reaching the top of the slope Brian staggered across the road to a telephone box. There was not a soul in sight, everyone was indoors enjoying Christmas and avoiding the torrential rain. Desperately trying to summon help, Brian tried again and again to lift the receiver and dial his parents' house for help. Eventually, despite the heavy bleeding and obvious pain, Brian managed to get through on the telephone to his father. Meanwhile his out-of-body self became aware of a huge bright light surrounding him and a comfortable floating sensation. He felt wonderful but at that point heard a voice telling him that he must go back, it was not yet his time to die. 'No,' was Brian's response. It all felt so marvellous that he wanted to stay. The light increased and he became aware of a spiralling sensation, followed by acute pain. It was clear to him that he was now back in his body, the shock and pain washing over him.

Almost at once he was aware of his father and wife bending over him and he could hear the approaching ambulance. Recovery was painfully slow and huge chunks of this period of time are lost to him. Like so many people who have had out-of-body experiences, this part of the incident is crystal-clear in Brian's memory. It was not to be the last time Brian would have a spiritual experience and we move several years ahead in Brian's life to when he was involved with writing music and playing with a band; he spent many hours in this pursuit with rather disastrous consequences.

> 'Never give up on anybody,
> miracles happen every day.'
> H. JACKSON BROWN JR

The social life of a band, as most people will know, often centres around alcohol. Unfortunately what started as harmless fun soon become essential to Brian's existence. He found that drinking was becoming a priority and although this was causing considerable distress to his wife, he seemed incapable of stopping. He realises in retrospect how selfish his dependency on alcohol made him and although he undoubtedly loved his wife dearly, no amount of pleading on her behalf made any difference. The inevitable happened: his wife asked him to leave. He was no longer the kind, loving man she had married and she could no longer cope with his behaviour. Sadly Brian left their lovely little cottage, located in the hills of the Scottish countryside, and moved into a miserable room in the city centre.

It was a very low point for Brian and although he desperately wanted to turn his life around, he had no idea how he might achieve it. One warm summer evening some time later, Brian drove to the little cottage intent on talking to his wife. He found her busy in the pretty garden but totally unresponsive to his request to talk. The pain was too deep and it was too soon for her to consider a heart-to-heart. Despondent, Brian decided to take a walk and try to clear his head; he felt the need to be alone. Leaving his car he walked up a path through the forest for a mile or so before pausing to reflect on the events of the day. Leaning on a gate, he felt the tears start to flow as he began to realise that he might have lost his wife for ever. Sobbing, he could not think what to do next but almost automatically he found himself praying. He spoke to God, asking for His help and pouring out the grief to Him. I really need a miracle, he thought, crying even louder. For twenty minutes or so he cried and prayed, letting out all his fears and emotions, until he felt totally exhausted.

Turning from the spot and slowly walking down the path, he became aware of what he can only describe as a loving presence. It was as if there was someone at his left shoulder. The presence was not at all frightening, and the thought went through his head that maybe this was his father who had passed away some time before. Instinct told him that this was not the case, and then suddenly he was physically lifted from his feet. Incredibly, he found himself virtually floating until he was gently placed back on the ground by a rowan tree. Decidedly confused, Brian looked around. He was completely alone in the forest, not a soul in sight nor a sound to be heard. There had been no voice, but he was certain that this again was an angelic presence. A flash of 'light and knowledge' filled his head at this point and it was as if he knew what he must do to turn his life around and regain the love and trust of his wife.

The rift was indeed healed and the couple was reunited. Resuming the musical career with his band, Brian now had his drinking well and truly behind him. At the end of one happy evening, the band had finished playing and Brian was preparing to load the equipment into his van. His wife had been to hear him play and would follow on in her car. Arriving at the cottage first Brian made a cup of tea and wandered into the bedroom, tired but pleased at the success of the night. Sipping his tea he listened for the sound of his wife's car outside, thankful for the happy life he had once more. The atmosphere in the room suddenly changed; there was an amazing feeling of all-embracing love. Slowly, almost as if in slow motion, Brian turned his head towards the bedroom door. Manifesting before his eyes was the most wonderful figure of an angel. The being was huge, hovering some two feet above the ground. The face was beautiful, and flowing from this being was pure love and peace. Wings stretched from above the angel's head to the floor and Brian calculated that the whole being must have been around eight feet tall. Slowly the vision faded, leaving Brian in a state of elation and wonder.

At last all was clear: this was the angel who had held him that evening on the forest road. The symbolism of being placed on another path was now so obvious. He had received the help and knowledge to restore his life. Everything was at last crystal-clear, it was as if he had been told 'well done' by the angel who had given him a second chance in life. How blessed and at peace he felt. He has tried to convey this feeling of harmony through his music and has composed a wonderful piece entitled 'Walking in Harmony'. I think that says it all!

People were streaming homeward at the end of the day, leaving their places of employment and emerging into the fine evening sunshine. It was warm and pleasant, so, having a little time to spare, Stephen decided to walk through the park. At 5 pm he assumed the park would be full of people enjoying the fine weather. Surprisingly, it was almost deserted, but all the more peaceful and pleasant for that fact. Little did Stephen realise that shortly the peace would be violently shattered.

From behind Stephen, with sickening speed, three figures sprang upon him. Launching a ferocious attack on him with no apparent motive, they rained blows on his head and torso relentlessly. To this day Stephen has no idea why, but it was the start of a nightmare. Blows to his face split the skin above his eye making visibility difficult and soon he found himself forced to the ground. The beating continued and he was roughly rolled through the undergrowth. The brambles tore into his skin and the kicks were forcing him to roll down a steep slope towards the lake. Immediately before hitting the water Stephen blacked out.

An amazing sequence of events followed, and they remain crystal-clear in Stephen's memory today, some four years later. He regained consciousness aware of a cooling breeze blowing on his forehead. Gentle fingers touched the spot above his injured right eye. A voice told him not to be afraid and then there was the sensation of a swift, soft kiss on his temple. 'You are completely safe,' said the voice. Opening his eyes wide, Stephen looked up and saw the most awesome sight. There was a figure floating approximately a foot above him and it appeared to taper into a white mist. The figure was all white, even the hair. Stephen felt that this figure was completely andro-gynous and that it radiated love and comfort.

The figure imparted some insights into many areas of knowledge, explaining that heaven was composed of six different planes. At this point Stephen was aware of loved ones who had died; their presence surrounded him. He was told emphatically by the angel that although he was with loved ones, he was not going to die; it was, the angel said, not his time. 'You are a young man with a wife and family to take care of and so you must return to them.' Like so many others in similar circumstances, Stephen wanted to stay in this wonderful glow of love and complete happiness. He heard his father, whom he had missed greatly since his death, tell him that some day they would be together. The angel told him that there was no such thing as time in the afterlife and whenever it was Stephen's time to die, his loved ones would be there waiting for him. The angel departed, leaving one more piece of knowledge, and that was to say everyone in heaven will find their true soulmate.

The incident remains etched upon Stephen's mind and yet he knows he has forgotten many more insights given to him at that time. The angel did say that he would be always near at hand and that if Stephen ever felt in need of him he had to ask for his friend. A lovely thought and lovely way to think of one's angel. A searing pain then shot through Stephen's body and he was aware of hands pulling him from the lake. Three policemen dragged him to safety. Cuts and scratches covered his now near-naked body and he was a sorry sight. He found it hard to believe that it was actually 6 am. How on earth could he have survived in the cold lake since the previous evening? Well, Stephen knew, of course, but he was reluctant to tell anyone and that is easy to understand! In time the injuries and scars healed and the mental trauma had been eliminated by the presence of the angel. From time to time Stephen does call on his 'special friend' and his presence is confirmed by the sensation of a warm glow. Stephen says the most important outcome of the whole incident is that he now has no fear whatsoever of death; in fact with such a friend he can face anything.

One of the most exciting events in any teenager's life must surely be passing the driving test. The sense of freedom when one can take to the road alone is quite wonderful. It is also the time that most parents start to worry anew: it is one more step to independence and one more cause for concern. Kathryn was feeling elated; she loved driving and it was quite wonderful to be able drive herself wherever she needed to go. Setting out one day soon after gaining her licence she drove along a road she had travelled several times before but never, however, alone. It presented some degree of difficulty. The width suddenly became restricted with a set of bollards on one side of the road and a metal bar on the other. The metal bar was actually on the driver's side and served to keep the vehicles off a set of large stone slabs.

Confidently approaching the road, Kathryn drove down it without reducing her speed. Arriving at the point where the road narrowed, she feels her inexperience caused her to over-compensate for the line of bollards and in a state of shock she hit the metal bar. There followed a horrendous crunching noise as the car slid along the ground, the driver's window and door coming into contact with the

41

hard surface. The huge stone slabs were now directly in her path and under these circumstances the result would be to hit one's head on the slabs. A fatality would surely be the result of such an accident. At this precise moment Kathryn had a very strange sensation: she felt totally protected and experienced overwhelming feelings of love and of unseen hands holding her head above the ground. There was no contact at all with the stones and she gradually came to a halt completely unhurt.

The sound of other cars stopping and their drivers rushing to Kathryn's aid brought her back to earth with a jolt. Willing hands forced open the passenger door and she was pulled clear. It was with total disbelief that witnesses saw she was unscathed and they failed to see how this could possibly be so. The only effect on Kathryn was one of incredulity and shock. This eventually gave way to the conviction that not only had she been saved by an angelic presence, but that the presence was someone very close to her. She realised in a flash that this was in fact her grandfather. When alive, Kathryn's grandfather and she had been very close; he was always protective towards her and she felt instinctively that he was taking care of her still. The hands holding her head away from fatal contact with those stone slabs were without a doubt, she says, those of her much loved grandfather.

✳ ✳ ✳ 2 ✳ ✳ ✳

Seeing is Believing

*'Tis only when they spring to heaven that angels
reveal themselves to you.'*

ROBERT BROWNING

Open any newspaper virtually any day in the week and you can guarantee there will be a story about the UK's favourite soap *Coronation Street*. Enquire of anyone about the current storyline and a pound to a penny they will be able to tell you. We are drawn to these characters, and all the trials and tribulations they endure on a weekly basis. They actually feel part of the fabric of our lives. At the end of the day, of course, the actors leave the studio and take up their real lives, where like everyone else they experience the joys and sorrows of day-to-day living.

For William Roache, *Coronation Street*'s Ken Barlow, there have been periods in his life when simple day-to-day living has become the biggest struggle and challenge he ever had to deal with. One evening seventeen years ago William and his wife prepared for a night out. They settled their little eighteen-month-old daughter, Edwina, in her cot, and kissed her goodnight. William's mother- and father-in-law had arrived to babysit. Peeping once more at the peacefully sleeping Edwina they happily set off for a pleasant night out.

Arriving home not too many hours later, they were told that Edwina appeared to be a little snuffly and was probably starting a cold. William went upstairs to check on her and it was true – she did sound as if a cold was coming but she was otherwise fine and still sleeping peacefully. Just one short hour later William's wife went to check on the little girl and to her horror discovered that she had stopped breathing. The shock was so great that they could scarcely take it in. They tried the kiss of life whilst waiting for the doctor and ambulance. Help arrived swiftly but a nightmare journey began as William and his wife followed the ambulance to hospital. How William functioned sufficiently to drive the car he can't imagine. The grief and pain were overwhelming and driving became purely automatic.

All attempts at resuscitation failed; their dear little daughter had died. How, they wondered, was it possible for a child to be well one minute and fatally ill the next? Gently the doctor explained to them that their little daughter had died of bronchial pneumonia. Sadly, the speed of this illness overwhelms the tiny bronchial tubes, with fatal results. It was not unknown in small children and there was no way William or his wife could have predicted what would happen.

The grief was so intense, William told me, that for the first time in his life he realised that emotional pain was synonymous with physical pain. His chest was gripped in an iron bar of pain, making breathing difficult. He was unable to speak or hold any conversation. Picking up the phone to make essential calls, he became wracked with sobs and words would not come. Neither William nor his wife were able to eat and for days existed only on mugs of hot chocolate. Mercifully they could talk to each other and found this terrible crisis bringing them closer.

Funerals are frequently highly charged, with everyone involved suffering and empathising with the loss. William dreaded the occasion, fearing he would not be able to cope. The days leading up to the funeral were a struggle and frequently he would collapse with the grief. The day of the funeral would be a culmination of this grief and he was convinced he would be unable to get through it.

The morning of the funeral dawned, and William lay in bed staring at the ceiling, unable to get up and face the day. It was then, as he reached his lowest point, that the most incredible event took place. In the corner of the bedroom a huge shining light appeared. William describes it as a glowing orb, radiating waves of love and comfort. Most wonderful of all, however, was the fact that there in the centre of this wonderful light was the face of his beloved Edwina. She was smiling and gazing directly towards him. He had this amazing secure feeling of knowing for certain she was perfectly happy and being cared for in the next world. Love surged through him and filled the room, giving him much needed support.

Opening her eyes, William's wife was aware of the love filling the room; it was palpable even though the vision had faded. 'I feel so much better,' William said. 'I know for certain I will be able to cope today.' His wife agreed, she too felt strengthened as they prepared for the events of the day. Indeed they did receive strength and survived the day without losing control and managing to find comfort in the funeral service.

William's father and grandfather were both doctors; he grew up in an atmosphere of intelligence and practical knowledge of science and medicine. He is not a fanciful man, but deeply spiritual with a keen understanding of philosophy and world religions. Edwina brought great love into his life, confirmation that love is central to living. He learned to let her go, sure in the knowledge that she is happy, understanding implicitly that we can never be separated from anyone even in death, as long as we continue to love them.

Topographically speaking, the English counties of Lancashire and Lincolnshire are very different. You cannot venture far in Lancashire before encountering steep gradients and finding yourself on the moors. Between the moors are deep valleys with rivers of soft water flowing through, which proved essential to the success of the cotton industry. By contrast, Lincolnshire has vast areas of flat farmland and woods, where walking and cycling are not too challenging.

David was born in Lancashire, but now lives in Lincolnshire. Travelling to see his family, he found the differences in terrain were marked. He often thought how much his father, who had recently suffered a severe stroke, would enjoy Lincolnshire. David's father, William, was not particularly good at taking care of himself. Lectures from his family on healthy eating and gentle exercise fell largely on deaf ears. As a consequence, William's health soon deteriorated.

A second stroke followed and this time William needed intensive medical care and attention. He was forced to move into a nursing home, where sadly he contracted pneumonia. His whole family, including David and his wife, quickly assembled at the nursing home. Hours passed and there was little change in his condition. Unsurprisingly everyone soon became hungry and it was decided that they would all go for a short time to a restaurant belonging to a family member.

Refreshed, the family returned to the nursing home. As they reached the entrance, David's sister hurried to catch up with the group. She declared happily, 'Father is much better, I have just seen him standing at the bedroom window upstairs.' Encouraged, they arrived at William's room, only to discover that he was in a deep coma. Minutes later William died, leaving everyone confused and shocked. David's sister, however, insisted that she had seen their father at the window.

David remained in Lancashire for the next few days until the funeral. It did occur to him and his wife that their neighbours might soon be a little concerned by their absence, but they had had no time to inform them of recent events. Their house was in a fairly secluded spot, and had a huge floor-to-ceiling plate-glass window in the living room, overlooking the road.

Sad and very weary, David and his family arrived home, the funeral very much on their minds. The lady from the house opposite greeted them with a look of confusion. She had, of course, wondered where they had been. David explained why they had stayed away so long. 'Who was the elderly gentleman,' she asked, 'taking care of the house in your absence? He sat in the lounge window gazing peacefully out each day.' Puzzled, David asked for a description and she furnished him with details. Open-mouthed, David realised that this was a perfect description of his father. The house bore no signs of forced entry or of anyone having stayed there. David remarked to his family that his father had apparently visited Lincolnshire after all. He has no doubt in his mind that his father is now an angel.

Christmas was coming and the shops were full of gifts. The same old songs filled the shopping centres. Coloured lights twinkled in the streets, heralding another festive season. However, it would not be a happy Christmas for Jessie: she had received the awful news that her mother was terminally ill. The thought of Christmas without her mother left her numb with grief, and feeling low both mentally and physically she succumbed to a severe bout of gastroenteritis and was confined to bed. On 17 December Jessie should have celebrated her birthday but she lay in bed in great pain, worrying about her mother. Worse was yet to come because on this day when all should have been jolly and filled with celebration, Jessie's mum died.

Several days later Jessie's grief was compounded by the fact that she was still so ill she was unable to attend her mother's funeral. There had been no chance to say goodbye or tell her how much she loved her.

Winter turned to summer and still Jessie worried – even on her holiday the anxiety would not go away. For some time a vein in her leg had been causing a great deal of pain. On holiday it became agony. When she returned home the doctor decided that the vein must be removed. In due course Jessie went into hospital for the operation. The procedure went smoothly and twenty-four hours later Jessie was sitting up in bed. There was some discomfort due to the throbbing in her leg and she concluded that sleep would be difficult. Refusing sleeping pills she declared her philosophy to be that it was preferable to avoid medication if at all possible. Night was approaching, the visitors had all gone home, and the ward fell strangely quiet. People were drifting off to sleep and one seriously ill lady appeared to be fading fast.

Pondering on this fact, Jessie started to worry anew. Had her mother died peacefully, without pain? How she wished she could have been with her to help and comfort in some way. Anxiety sweeping through her, she wondered if these events would ever be soothed in her mind. It was at this point that the most astonishing event in Jessie's life took place. Walking down the ward looking solid and real was her mother! Indistinguishable from any other person in the ward, she was dressed in normal familiar clothing and walked purposefully up to Jessie's bed. Halting at the foot of the bed she looked directly into Jessie's eyes. Smiling she said, 'You must stop worrying. I wish you to understand that I am fine. I am happy and at peace and you must be also. Please do not worry.' From that day to this Jessie has never worried about her mother again.

I know quite a few grandmothers – one drives a fast red sports car whilst another is a company director. One particularly energetic grandmother is a national swimming champion, spending most of her spare time coaching young swimmers for competitions. They love their grandchildren and thoroughly enjoy spending time with them, but they are far removed from the image of grandmothers sitting in a rocking chair knitting.

Margaret was perhaps nearer the old image than most. She lived with her daughter and son-in-law and of course her much loved grandchildren. It was a wonderfully happy arrangement. Always on hand, full of wisdom but never imposing opinions, she was involved in all the family activities by invitation and considerably added to the happy atmosphere of the household. Two main activities attracted this family. Firstly they loved walking, and immensely enjoyed exploring the countryside around their leafy Sussex home. Secondly they were passionately fond of card-games. Most Saturdays they would play cards all evening, and were always joined by their dear friends James and Mavis for much laughter and many games of whist etc. This had become a weekly ritual enjoyed by all.

The family regarded James and Mavis as 'aunt and uncle' whilst they in turn adopted the grandmother as theirs!

One beautiful summer evening James and Mavis were getting ready to visit when they received a phone call from their friends. Margaret had been taken ill and was on her way by ambulance to the local hospital. They were assured that they would keep them informed of any developments. Much to everyone's distress, later that evening the dear old lady died. It was hard to imagine life without Margaret in the family. James and Mavis felt the sadness compounded by the fact that they had not had the opportunity to say goodbye. They would miss her dreadfully and how they regretted not having had the chance to tell her how loved she was.

A week or so after the funeral, Mavis received a call to say that the following Saturday they would be happy to see them as usual for their card night. It was thought that Margaret would approve and not wish them to give up their happy evenings. Greeted warmly by the family, Mavis thought how lovely it was to be together again. Stepping into the spacious hall, Mavis looked down the corridor towards the kitchen. There in the doorway, smiling as broadly as ever, stood Margaret! Plain as daylight and wearing a very familiar dress that she had been particularly fond of. It was fairly obvious to Mavis that no one else could see her because everyone walked past the figure into the lounge. She decided not to speak of this but as she approached the spot where Margaret stood the figure slowly faded. There was a distinct sensation of a hand on hers as she walked past into the lounge.

The family sat around the card table in their usual places. Someone remarked how strange it felt not to have Margaret with them. 'She is,' said James. 'I have just seen her as I came down the hall. She was wearing that lovely blue and white dress she so often wore.' Everyone fell silent but soon recovered and the evening went ahead. Speaking about it to each other later, Mavis revealed that she too had seen Margaret. It was fairly obvious that she had come to say goodbye.

Every English village has its characters, usually eccentric and mostly well loved. Anne's village was no exception, and the most colourful of its characters was old Mrs Bray. For as long as anyone could remember Mrs Bray had owned the village sweet shop. Often Anne would pop into the shop perhaps only to buy a paper and would emerge with a handful of sweets pressed on her as a gift for her three boys. It seemed to be an indisputable fact that Mrs Bray gave away more than she sold, but the twinkle in her eye made one realise that this was her way of spreading love.

The little village church was central to Mrs Bray's life since the death of Mr Bray. She loved the choir and sang with enthusiasm, swaying to the music and putting her whole heart into the hymns. She was indeed well known and well loved and when she was not serving in her shop or singing in church she could be seen trundling along the main street pulling her shopping trolley behind her. Smiling and chatting to all she met, she was part and parcel of village life.

As she had been living alone for many years, kindly neighbours kept a watchful eye out for her. Anne was particularly concerned one day to discover that she had been taken into hospital. The strange sight of the closed shop with it shutters down had alerted Anne and she was sad to learn that poor Mrs. Bray had been taken ill. Telling herself that it was just as well that she was in fact admitted to hospital, Anne drove home content that the old lady was receiving the best treatment.

Several days passed and everyone missed the gentle old lady with the twinkle in her eye. All wished her a speedy recovery. Driving to work one morning, Anne passed the sweet shop and slowly approached the traffic lights in the centre of the village street. From this vantage point at the crossroads the whole of the village could be seen. Waiting for the red light to change Anne sat taking in the scene. Suddenly to her delight she spotted Mrs Bray coming down the street towards her. She was pulling her familiar wheeled shopping trolley behind her and Anne thought what a welcome sight it was. Pulling away past the familiar figure Anne thought she must have been shopping and was on her way back to the little shop, sprightly as ever. How wonderful to have her back, Anne thought. I shall pop in to see her shortly after work.

After the evening meal Anne's friend dropped in for a chat and a cup of tea. The friends sat at the kitchen table to catch up on the news. 'Did you hear about Mrs Bray?' Anne's friend enquired. 'Well yes,' replied Anne, 'it's wonderful to have her home so quickly. I saw her this morning as I drove to work, trundling her trolley as usual.'

Open-mouthed the friend stared at her. 'What's the matter?' Anne asked. The reply drained the colour from Anne's cheeks. 'She died yesterday,' her friend said. There was not a shadow of doubt in Anne's mind that she had seen Mrs Bray, she was so near and crystal-clear in every detail. She must have been having one last look around her beloved village, Anne thought.

∗ ∗ 3 *∗ ∗*

Comfort in Times of Stress

'Angels represent God's personal care for each
one of us.'
FR. ANDREW GREELEY

Fifty years is a long time to be married. It always
seems to me that when the institution of marriage
became established 'till death us do part' probably
indicated twenty years together at the most. The average
life span was so much shorter it was unlikely that anyone
would reach their three score years and ten. With amazing
medical advances and good nutrition we are living a good
deal longer than three score and ten in most cases. This
being the case, sustaining a happy marriage for fifty years
can be regarded as quite an achievement. Alice and Arthur
had loved and respected one another all those years and still
enjoyed each other's company a great deal. It was then a
great pleasure for their children and grandchildren to plan
a huge golden wedding party.

What a splendid occasion it was – lots of guests, a
wonderful cake and champagne for the toast. An evening
meal to suit every palate was followed by live music. Alice

had been a little concerned about the choice of music her family might have arranged but she need not have worried because, interspersed with the modern pop for the youngsters, were all their old favourites. It was without doubt a night to remember and the pleasure of poring over the photographs afterwards was immense. Flowers and cards filled the little house and the couple felt truly blessed.

Imagine the distress when, only a few short weeks later, Arthur suffered a heart attack and died almost instantly. Alice and her family were devastated and yet she could see how fortunate she had been to have enjoyed so many happy years. It would, she knew, take a long time to pick up the pieces and be a real effort to live alone for the first time in her life. Autumn turned to winter and Alice ploughed on, showing a brave face to the world. It was the long, cold dark evenings that presented the biggest challenge, when she felt terribly lonely. On one particularly dark evening, Alice decided to go to bed early with a book and try to read although she knew it would not be easy.

Concentrating was decidedly difficult and she seemed to have little interest in most things. After some time trying to read without success, Alice closed her book and said with a loud sigh, 'Oh Arthur, I do miss you.' To her astonishment the side of the bed where Arthur had always slept suddenly moved. A deep depression appeared as if someone had just sat firmly upon it. No bright light, no angels to be seen, but Alice was filled with joy. Arthur has not gone far away after all, she thought.

Light has always been associated with the divine and goodness, whilst evil and all things bad are represented by the dark. Even on the very basic level of cowboy films, as a child one learns quickly that the cowboy dressed in white is the hero, the one in black the villain. Unsurprisingly therefore, many out-of-body experiences, near-death experiences and angelic encounters feature a bright light. People on the brink of death will often describe a light of intense brightness that does not hurt the eyes at all. This light radiates feelings of love and comfort and has become known as 'the being of light'. The light is often described as 'the angel of death' when specifically related to imminent departure from this world. The term is I feel quite frightening and I think 'the angel of greeting' would be more appropriate. Often loved ones at the bedside will be asked if they can see this being and feel the love. It is a comfort to the ones left behind to feel that the person on the brink of the next world is not alone. Certainly Jill felt this way. Here is her story.

The consultant had been kind but truthful, telling Jill and her husband that there was in fact no treatment available that would extend her husband's life. Pain control would be administered and every care extended towards him in the pursuit of comfort. The illness was not only terminal but the prognosis was that he could expect only a few months of life.

In the event a few months proved to be an optimistic prognosis. The disease accelerated to the point where in only six weeks from diagnosis, Jill's husband Peter was admitted to a hospice. The most distressing aspect of this was the fact that Peter was very afraid of dying. He was not a religious man and had never thought about the afterlife, or indeed considered whether there was one. It was a subject for contemplation later in life, he thought, never imagining that he would have to face dying at the age of forty years.

All too soon the final stage of his illness arrived and Jill sat holding Peter's hand, trying to calm and comfort him. Jill silently started to pray, something she had not done since the days of Sunday School. Please God, she asked, help Peter. Tears fell down her face and she felt helpless in the face of such fear. Suddenly a calm expression spread over Peter's face. Opening his eyes wide he turned to Jill and said, 'Look, there they are.' Jill could see nothing but nodded bravely. 'They are so beautiful,' said Peter. 'It is the first time I have ever seen angels.' 'Can you see the light?' Jill asked. 'Oh yes,' he replied. 'It is so very bright but does not hurt at all.' Instinctively Jill told him to reach for the light. Slowly sinking his head into the pillow and with a large sigh, he was gone. If a death could be described as beautiful, Jill thought, then that certainly was. She knew her prayers had been answered. Peter had lost his fear and was now at last in God's care.

Working as an au pair in London was proving to be a very pleasant experience for Maria. She had committed herself to twelve months with the family, taking care of two little girls and helping with household chores. In return she was allowed time to study and she would have the pleasure of travelling with the family. She did miss her home and family in France, especially in the first few weeks. It was especially difficult to leave her boyfriend, even though they had met only shortly before Maria's departure for England. The channel tunnel made visiting easy and they would meet, he promised, at least once a month. Letters and phone calls helped and before she knew it the months were slipping by. Christmas was fast approaching and the family allowed Maria to go home to Paris.

What a wonderful Christmas is was for Maria. Catching up with family and friends and of course spending lots of time with Marcel, her boyfriend. It was agreed that on Maria's return she would share an apartment with her sister to enable her to be nearer Marcel and, with that happy prospect in mind, she returned to England to complete her year. Soon she was home again and quickly acquired a job which utilised her English language skills. It was such a happy time, close to Marcel and having the freedom of an apartment, especially as Maria's sister travelled a great deal, her job taking her all over France.

One day Maria's happy life came crashing down around her. She received a phone call announcing the awful news of Marcel's sudden death. He had suffered a cerebral haemorrhage, believed to be from a congenital defect. Poor Maria could scarcely take in the news – it was impossible to think of the lively, fun-loving young man as dead. Struggling through the following weeks was a nightmare and Maria felt as if the whole thing was unreal and that soon she would wake to find all was back to normal.

Not having had an opportunity to say goodbye was a great source of distress also, and she often felt quite numb with grief. One bitter cold day she wrapped up warmly and made her way to the cemetery, feeling a strong need to talk to Marcel. I know this is illogical, she thought, but I need to tell him how I feel and to say goodbye. She told him that her message to him was that she hoped the angels were taking care of him, and she explained how awful it was not to have said goodbye or to have had a message from him in return. Feeling much better she made her way back to the little apartment, shivering with cold but feeling warm inside. Walking into the kitchen to make a hot drink, she was stopped in her tracks by a puzzling sight. There in the middle of the kitchen table was a small ceramic angel! It certainly had not been there when she left and her sister was away for another two days. Only she had a key and clearly no one had been in the room except herself. Tears ran down her face; this surely had to be the message she had longed for. Marcel was with the angels, but they were obviously taking care of her also.

Airports represent different emotions to different people. Some time ago I was waiting in line, boarding pass in hand, preparing to leave New York and fly to Manchester. At the front of the queue was a lady with her little daughter, possibly five or six years old. The child was extremely distressed, declaring loudly that she did not want to go on the plane. Her cries became louder the nearer she came to the aircraft and she was clearly very frightened. Talking to the child calmly and trying to reassure her, the mother told her that there was nothing to be afraid of. She reminded the little girl that they were going to visit grandparents in England and how lovely that would be. All to no avail, the child was inconsolable. Settling into their seats, passengers exchanged glances that said, it's going to be a long flight!

Half an hour or so into the flight, the pilot, on hitting turbulence, advised everyone to sit in their seats and fasten their safety belts. The turbulence merely added to the child's distress and the poor mother redoubled her efforts to calm her. Realising that the seat in front, which contained a small television screen, was about to show a Disney film, she feverishly tried to find it. Twiddling the knobs and dials on the arm of her seat she flicked through the available channels. Sobbing loudly, the child looked through the window, where she had been seated in an effort to amuse her with the view. 'Look, Mummy,' she suddenly shouted, 'there's an angel outside the window.' 'Yes, dear,' replied her mother, not paying attention and still trying to find the right channel. 'I'm going to be all right now,' the child said. 'The angel will look after me.' Several people said, 'Aah,' and I longed to be able to peep through the window. Willing her mother to pay attention and take a look, I was intrigued to know if she could see anything outside the window. At last the mother found the children's film on the screen and settled back with relief, telling her daughter how much fun the film would be. The turbulence ceased, everything was back to normal. What of the little girl, you might ask. Well, she was good as gold all the way to Manchester.

Major life changes are frequently difficult to cope with. When these changes are forced upon us they can be a traumatic experience. After many happily married years Sylvia found the death of her husband hard to bear. In addition to this loss, she realised that she would have to move from the family home. The house was too big and too financially draining for one person. Her family was very supportive and understood her dilemma.

Eventually a nice, suitable little house was found and Sylvia moved in. Although she realised only too well that this was the most sensible course of action, it was nevertheless very painful. Everything felt strange and unfamiliar and she was most conscious that her life was entering a new phase. Overwhelmed from time to time by feelings of isolation and loneliness, she bravely battled on. One winter's night Sylvia was feeling very low in spirits and physically cold. She pulled the sofa nearer to the fire and, with a feeling of despondency sweeping over her, she said aloud, 'How will I ever cope?'

At this instant the atmosphere in the room changed and Sylvia was aware of a presence. The room filled with a sensation of love; it was almost palpable. Most wonderful of all, Sylvia felt strong arms gently encircling her and for some time they held her tight. There was, of course, no one in the room except Sylvia. In Sylvia's mind, it was without question her husband. He was communicating to her that she was not and never would be alone. It really did not matter where she lived, he would never be far away. Years later Sylvia can still close her eyes and summon up the feeling of those gentle arms; she has faced the future with courage and leads a full life, confident in the knowledge that she is never alone.

'Spiritual love is a position of standing with one hand extended into the universe and one hand into the world, letting ourselves be a conduit for passing energy.'
CHRISTINA BALDWIN

For many of us, childhood can be the happiest time of our lives. Memories of sunshine and laughter predominate even though the time is often remembered through rose-coloured glasses. It can be a confusing time also and many people have less than happy memories of this period. Half-understood facts and situations cause worry and concern and are often difficult for the child to articulate. At the age of eight years, Carol had the worries and insecurities of a

much older child. Carol's mother suffered dreadfully with
arthritis and would frequently be forced to spend long
periods in hospital. Carol would worry about her mother
dying and inferred that these long hospital spells would
result in her death. The whole subject of death and dying
started to dominate Carol's thoughts and she found it
difficult to talk to anyone about this.

During one of her mother's extended stays in hospital it
was decided that Carol would stay with her aunt. This
pleased Carol immensely as she was very fond of the aunt
and also of the lovely large house where she lived. It was a
large, old house and had a special atmosphere that made
Carol feel very comfortable. The sensation was difficult to
define but she felt at peace and cared for in that safe
environment. The days passed happily and Carol enjoyed
her aunt's company. In spite of this she still found herself
mulling over the issues of life and death. Carol laughed
when she told me the next part of the story, but I feel it
would be logical for an eight-year-old to sit in a dog kennel!
She wanted a quiet place where she could be completely
alone and a spot where no one would think of looking for
her. The dog kennel was the obvious choice to her and the
dog obligingly vacated it for her. Tucked away at the end of
the garden in solitude she found herself once more deep in
thought. To her surprise she had the distinct feeling that she
was not alone; a wonderful feeling of love surrounded her
and she felt completely at peace. It was a feeling she had
yearned for without even understanding what the meaning
of the word was. A sweet, kind voice then spoke to her.
She was told that she was not to worry, many things would

be made clear to her when she was older and she would then fully understand. At last her worries and confusion ceased and she had the most wonderful feeling that she would never be alone. It was a remarkable experience for one so young but even at that age she knew that the experience had been spiritual and came to the conclusion that the voice had been that of an angel.

Her faith in the angels would be sorely tested in the years to come but for the present Carol was at peace. From the age of eleven, the quiet, beautiful countryside of Lincolnshire became her home and the family settled into a very English village life. Of all her friends in this village there was one special person whom Carol related to. It was a young boy of similar age and they found that they could chat about anything under the sun. It was good fun to have a 'best friend' and Carol was very happy. The only blot on the horizon was the fear that her father might be moved with his job and they all hoped that this would not happen. Eventually when Carol was fifteen years old the news she had been dreading arrived. Her father was to be transferred to Dorset. It seemed a world away, but also on a very practical level it was most inconvenient – this was the year that Carol was to sit her O-Level examinations. Everything looked black to Carol. One evening she sat on her bed and sobbed; how she would miss her friends, school and particularly her very closest friend.

This was a terrible blow and she did not know what to do; she was quite inconsolable. Looking up, she became aware of a strong bright light pouring through the window. The most amazing feature of this light, however, was the fact that it projected the shadow of a cross on her bedroom wall. How this could possibly be, Carol could not imagine. Her window did not have a crossbar and when she got out of bed and moved the curtains, the shadow did not move. There was no apparent source of this light from outside and she watched transfixed as the shadow and the light slowly faded. Once more the overwhelming feeling of support and love filled the room and she knew again that she was not alone.

To everyone's delight the following morning a solution to the predicament presented itself. A kind neighbour offered a place in her home, enabling Carol to stay in the village and complete her examinations in familiar surroundings. Staying close to her special friend was also a huge relief and she could not have been happier. However, when Carol's parents moved it was still quite a wrench. Mixed emotions ran through Carol – she felt on the one hand quite grown-up because she was approaching the age of sixteen, but also very vulnerable. It was, she says, in retrospect rather inevitable that she would become ever closer to her special friend. The transition from friend to boyfriend occurred swiftly with rather unfortunate results. Carol became pregnant.

Perhaps the most unfortunate part of this was the fact that Carol had no idea of her condition. It frequently happens in the very young that the usual signs and symptoms are not evident. Carol carried on a normal life oblivious to the drama about to unfold. 'Puppy fat' is only too common at this age and everyone ignored Carol's increasing size, including Carol herself. One day, for the first time in her life, Carol woke with severe back pain. Totally confused by this she visited the doctor. After examining her, the doctor told a bemused Carol that she was in an advanced stage of pregnancy! In fact this was just five short days away from the baby's arrival. Her parents had to be informed and Carol must travel to be with them in Dorset.

Telling her parents was every bit as horrific as she had predicted. They were angry, resentful and bitterly disappointed in her and Carol felt distraught. The kindly doctor tried to point out to them that Carol, having been unaware of her condition until very late into the pregnancy, had not been taken care of. All the usual ante-natal care and advice had been missing and Carol really needed peace and quiet to prepare for the delivery. This was not to be and she was told in no uncertain terms that the baby must instantly be handed over to the adoption services. Carol was beside herself at the thought of giving her baby away – the thought had not entered her head.

Soon labour began and her father drove her to the hospital. At this point Carol's mother had chosen to completely cut herself off from the situation. Reeling from the shock, the sixteen-year-old found herself in a strange environment, in pain and completely alone. The hospital staff were kind but incredibly busy and not able to spend time with Carol before it was absolutely necessary. A sympathetic nurse told Carol not to worry, it would be some time before the baby was born and she would be back to see her later. Although Carol had obviously never been in this situation before everything indicated to her that the little one would be there very quickly. She was terrified, alone in the little room and feeling alone in the world. She started to pray, fervently asking God to help her. Looking out of the window towards the harbour, she became aware of an unusual light shining outside her window and appearing to cover all the harbour with its glow. She was then filled with the most fantastic feeling of calm and peace, and was instantly comforted. The sensation was one of love being poured over and around her, shielding her from any harm or worry. There was the sense of a deeply loving presence and she felt marvellous.

Calmly summoning the nurse she announced that the birth was imminent. Extremely surprised, the nurse confirmed her prediction to be accurate. In no time at all and without complication a little girl was born. The nurse told Carol that she was a very brave young lady. Carol knew with her inner peace and her natural determination that no matter what she would never give her baby for adoption. The love she felt for this little girl was so very powerful and she knew that in the most stressful time of her young life she had been helped once more by God's messengers and love. Surely, she reasoned, I shall not be deserted and I shall raise my daughter. After long discussions, her parents eventually relented and allowed her to keep the baby. Today Carol has a lovely adult daughter who has brought love and life to Carol in abundance.

No parents expect to outlive their children; it feels totally against the natural order and is an abhorrent thought. Sadly, however, some people have to cope with this dreadful loss.

A close bond had existed between Josie and her son Philip. He, his wife and two small sons lived fairly close to her, enabling Josie to see them frequently. She was happy to help in the daily care of the two little boys. The distress they all felt when Philip was diagnosed to be suffering from cancer was enormous. The cancer proved to be virulent and invasive, treatment failed to halt its rapid progress and soon Philip was very ill indeed. More chemotherapy was suggested, but due to the fact that several secondary tumours had been detected it was decided by the medical team and Philip to reject further treatment. Sadly, in a short space of time Philip died.

Death produces many emotions in the grieving family, they range from disbelief to anger and all are perfectly natural reactions. Josie felt a great deal of anger; she even wished Philip had tried more treatment, exploring every avenue before being defeated. She can see in retrospect that this would in all likelihood have been futile. It was just one way of expressing her anger and grief.

Sitting by his grave one day, Josie felt the anger welling up inside her along with the overwhelming feeling of loneliness at his loss. I wonder if I shall ever see him again, she thought. Wearily she made her way home, the feeling of desolation accompanying her. The house seemed very empty, though she had in fact grown accustomed to living alone and very rarely felt isolated. Later that night she sat in bed, unable to shake off her depressing feelings, when odd things started to happen. She felt as if she was almost in a trance-like state, not asleep but not fully awake. She could hear voices although she knew that the house was empty apart from herself. There was a sensation of being touched, a hand on her bare shoulder was accompanied by the room filling with a wonderful glowing light. From that time also, her dreams became extremely lucid and symbolic. It all added up to the fact that she was being contacted by Philip, who clearly wanted her to let go of her anger and to reassure her that he was not far away.

Josie is a healer – she practises Reiki – and from that time onwards she was acutely aware of a presence behind her when giving treatment. It was yet another confirming experience that helped Josie cope with her anger and grief. Talking with a close friend about these incidents she said that her anger had subsided and she felt convinced that Philip was now free from pain and worry. 'Let him go then,' advised the friend. 'He has achieved what he wanted for you.' Josie found herself saying, 'Thank you, Philip, I shall be fine now.' The process of letting her anger go and also of letting her son go was very liberating. From time to time she still feels his presence and knows she will always have an angel at her shoulder.

At the age of ninety-four Grandma Robson was very frail. She had enjoyed a long and very active life, rarely succumbing to illness and enjoying the reputation of being 'as tough as old boots'. She was now literally winding down and everything seemed to be failing at once. She still derived great pleasure from the visits of her family, especially her great-grandchildren. So often the very young and the very old have a unique affinity and this was certainly true of Grandma Robson and her dear little family members. The doctor decided against taking Grandma Robson to hospital; he reasoned that there was little that they could do except make her comfortable. Her considerable family volunteered to look after her and see to her needs in the comfort of her own home. It was difficult for her now to leave the confines of her bed but the constant stream of visitors, far from tiring her, seemed to make her very happy.

Despite all this care it was clear to all that the end was very near and on one occasion all her sons and daughters, who numbered six, arrived at the same time. Janet was one of the twenty grandchildren and, on what was to be Grandma Robson's last day, she arrived with her little daughter Amy. Grandma was as ever pleased to see them, but shortly after they arrived her breathing became very laboured and speech difficult. Janet took Amy downstairs and called her mother and the doctor. Both were there very quickly and in no time at all the doctor said that Grandma Robson had simply slipped away. Janet's mother said that she had actually looked very happy, a smile spreading across her face immediately before she died.

Later that evening when little Amy was being read a bedtime story, she started to ask about Grandma Robson and heaven. Janet explained as carefully as she could that Grandma would now be with all the people she loved who had gone to heaven before her. 'Will the little girl be with her?' Amy asked. 'Which little girl?' Janet said. 'The one sitting by her bed when we went downstairs,' was the reply. 'She had a lovely white dress on and a large ribbon in her hair.' Janet did not know what to think and decided it was Amy's imagination. In the kitchen Janet's mother was making a cup of tea and silently crying. On seeing Janet she told her that she was wondering if in fact Grandma was amongst loved ones after all. Telling her Amy's story to take her mind off the problem Janet was taken aback when her mother started to cry even louder. 'Whatever is the matter?' she asked. Her mother explained, when she had calmed a little, that Grandma's first child was a little girl who had died at the age of four. Amy's description of the child at the bedside fitted the little girl exactly. 'There is the answer to your question then,' said Janet. 'I cannot begin to tell you what a comfort it is,' Janet's mother declared, peacefully sipping her tea.

Linda was finding it very difficult to sleep. It was a rather stuffy summer night, but more than that, her brain refused to switch off. All day she had been feeling uneasy and decidedly unwell. It was difficult to identify the source of this uneasy feeling, but the birth of her baby would be any day now and she felt the anxiety was attributable to this. All kinds of aches and pains make life uncomfortable at this stage, but she felt an anxiety unlike any previously experienced. Giving up completely on the idea of sleep, she got out of bed and softly went downstairs, not wishing to wake her husband. Pouring a glass of milk, she walked through to the lounge and opened a window, hoping to catch a breeze.

Through the window came more than a breeze; a bright radiating light filled the room and within the light a figure slowly became clear. It was without doubt, Linda said, an angel. No wings or iridescent robes of white, but a face so beautiful and loving that Linda could only stare in awe.

The figure stayed only a few short moments, but it felt like a lifetime. What was she to make of it, Linda asked herself. Why me? I really thought angels were for those in danger, she mused. Returning to bed, she fell into a deep, refreshing sleep. The following day, labour pains began and Linda and her husband drove to the hospital. It was a worrying time and it became clear shortly after their arrival that all was not well. Despite the efforts of the medical team, the baby died. There followed a period of great distress for all the family; a little baby girl had been given and so quickly taken from them.

Arriving home from the hospital, Linda sat talking to her mother and found herself relating the events of the night before the birth. 'One of the most frightening things about this situation,' she told her mother, 'is wondering if the baby has gone to heaven. I now know exactly why the angel appeared that night. She was telling me that she had come to take my little girl to heaven where she would look after her.' In the midst of her grief, Linda discovered a great blessing.

Everyday Angels

See I am sending an angel ahead of you to guard you along the way.

Occasionally I am contacted for my opinion about some incident which on the face of it is quite ordinary but contains extraordinary elements. The only explanation appears to be help from some angelic source. When I happily confirm that I have a huge file of similar encounters, the delight and relief is almost palpable. The following story is fairly typical of these seemingly ordinary events. The Bible also tells us that we often maybe entertaining angels unawares (Hebrews 13: 1–2).

Heather and Periky had travelled to London for a course connected to their careers. The first morning brought the realisation that they would have to cross London and find the building in an unfamiliar area. It seemed a daunting task and the girls were apprehensive. The Underground train was crowded and stuffy, decidedly unpleasant. Everyone had their heads deeply thrust into newspapers and books, avoiding eye contact. Suddenly a young man jumped up with a comforting smile and offered his seat. This alone was a minor miracle on a Monday morning. It was a welcome gesture and both girls were struck by the unusual nature of his piercing blue eyes. Feeling a little less anxious they continued their journey. Alighting at the correct station, their cheerfulness evaporated as they realised that they had no idea how to find the building where the course was being held. In their haste and confusion, the directions had been left behind in the hotel room.

Riding upwards on the very steep escalator they were surprised to be approached at the top by another gentleman. 'Are you lost?' he enquired. Without waiting for a reply he urged them to follow him. Mesmerised, they did so and soon found themselves weaving through very unfamiliar, busy streets. Halting suddenly at a large building he said cheerfully, 'There you are.' To their delight they realised that they were indeed standing outside the very building they needed. Shouting thank you to the hastily departing figure they felt sheer relief at having arrived on time. It was at this point that they turned to each other open-mouthed and said, 'How on earth did he know where we were going?' No one had told him, they had never seen him before in their lives and they certainly were not carrying a file or stationery displaying the address. Secondly, this man also had the most piercing blue eyes, identical to the man's on the train, plus the same knowing smile. Could this possibly have been angelic help, they mused. Deep down inside they already knew the answer.

Opera lovers everywhere will identify with the excitement
Caroline felt at the possibility of an evening at the Royal
Opera House in London's Covent Garden. 'Othello' was
to be the opera and Placido Domingo the star tenor, both
Caroline's favourites. Accompanied by a friend, she stood
in a queue one Saturday afternoon outside the Opera
House, waiting to purchase tickets. All the signs were that
it would be a long wait and Caroline was not feeling too
well. A migraine headache was worsening and she
reluctantly left her friend to make her way home. The most
obvious route would have been via the Tube train but the
thought of the hot crowded carriages prompted Caroline to
walk in the fresh air for a while. It was possible to walk to
Waterloo Station and take an overland train from there.
Waves of nausea hit Caroline as she made her way to the
Embankment. A cool breeze felt very refreshing and as she
walked by the River Thames she did start to feel a little
better. It was winter and the lights of the Festival Hall
twinkled in the early evening darkness.

Her newly found cheerfulness was soon dashed by the
realisation that after walking across Waterloo Bridge she
must now face the area known as the Bullring. It was an
underpass through which she must walk to reach the train
station and the prospect was quite frightening. She felt every
sympathy for the homeless who were forced to live in this
area, but she knew with a sinking heart that many would be
under the influence of alcohol or drugs. The frightening
thought for Caroline was that these people were not in control of their actions. There was no going back, she reasoned
– it was much too far and she would just have to be brave.

It was by now quite dark and the lighting in the underpass was poor. Caroline found herself praying silently, 'Please, God, help me.' Forcing herself to walk forward she saw about twenty people huddled together in the gloom. Stepping quickly into the area she was suddenly surprised and delighted to see another woman walking a little way ahead of her. Well, she thought, there's safety in numbers, and hurried a little to try to catch her up. On almost reaching her she noticed that the lady was quite young and walking calmly and purposefully straight ahead. Tall and slim, the young lady exuded confidence and Caroline tucked in behind her as she walked. She must be able to hear my footsteps, Caroline thought, but she did not turn around.

The narrow area was crowded with people drinking and lurching from one side to the other, waving bottles in the air. No one approached them or, stranger still, asked for money. It was as if the two women could not actually be seen. Mercifully the stairs leading to Waterloo Station soon came into view; the ordeal will soon be over, Caroline thought. Just ahead of her the tall young lady mounted the steps, her shoes echoing loudly on the stone stairs. There were only two steps to climb before the stairs turned to the left and there then followed a long straight stretch up to the top. As Caroline reached the bottom stair she heard the lady turn to walk up the long straight section. Hearing her footsteps clearly Caroline hurried to say thank you for being such a support and staying so calm. Quickly turning to the left she was awe-struck to find the staircase completely empty! The lady had simply disappeared. She could not possibly have reached the top without being seen, Caroline was after all only seconds behind her and could still hear her footsteps. The staircase had steep, concrete sides – it was impossible for anyone to have vaulted over them. Swiftly arriving at the top of the stairs Caroline was even more confused; there was no one in sight in any direction. Impossible though it was there was only one conclusion to be reached and that was to face the fact that a lady had vanished almost literally in front of her eyes.

Arriving home safely Caroline went over the events of the evening in her mind. It then seemed to her that God had in fact answered her prayer for help. Not all angels are dressed in white and surrounded by a glow – how inappropriate that would have been in those surroundings. Surely that had been an everyday angel, leading her to safety on that dark, dangerous night.

> '*All God's angels come to us disguised.*'
> JAMES RUSSELL LOWELL

The train from Manchester to Euston arrived twenty minutes late, a fairly common occurrence – Graham was relieved it had not taken longer. If he could catch a taxi fairly swiftly he would still make his meeting on time. Dashing across the concourse and down the stairs to the taxi rank his heart sank slightly when he saw the length of the queue. It did move fairly quickly however and soon he was speeding across London as fast as the traffic would allow. Climbing from the taxi with his overnight bag and smart suit in a carrier he entered the hotel. How very elegant, he thought, and it hit him again that he was representing his company at a very important meeting and also on duty at a business dinner that evening.

Signing in at the front desk, he was asked if he needed help with the luggage up to his room. Lifting his bag from the floor he suddenly felt a wave of nausea sweep over him; he did not have his briefcase! All the important papers for the meeting were inside it – what on earth could he do? Thinking as clearly as he could under the circumstances, he realised that he must have left it on the train in his rush to get a taxi. Perhaps he should ring Euston to see if it had been found, he thought, and was about to ask the receptionist if he might use the phone. His hands were shaking, as he realised that the meeting was due to start in the conference room in just half an hour.

Whilst dialling the number he became aware of a gentle tugging at his sleeve. Looking down he saw a white-haired old man with the deepest blue eyes smiling at him. 'I think this must belong to you,' he said and, incredibly, handed Graham his precious briefcase. Transfixed to the spot with shock and relief, Graham could only mouth 'thank you' – his voice had deserted him with the stress of the situation. Calmly the old man raised his hand in farewell and slowly left the hotel.

Seconds later, as if waking from a spell, Graham bounded through the hotel front door after the man. He was nowhere to be seen. From the top of the hotel steps

Graham could see in both directions and although the pavement was slightly busy with people, there was no sign of his old gentleman. How on earth could he have vanished in seconds, Graham thought. He was terribly sad not to have thanked him properly; he would have liked to tell him just how important the meeting was for him and how the man had literally saved the day.

Later, when he had calmed down, Graham was even more puzzled. Where had the old man come from? How did he know it was his briefcase? If he had found it on the train why did he not follow him to the taxi rank where he had stood for a little time waiting? Could this man possibly have followed him in a taxi to the hotel? It was all so improbable. To add to the puzzle Graham distinctly recalls seeing the old gentleman inside the hotel lobby as he entered. How could he possibly have known he was going to be at that particular hotel? The facts simply did not add up, and days spent wrestling with them followed. The meeting proved to be highly successful for Graham and he was filled with a feeling of gratitude. He came to the following conclusion. The sensation of being spellbound when handed the briefcase had produced a rather unworldly feeling. The calm presence of the man with the piercing blue eyes convinced him that he had in fact encountered his guardian angel.

Meeting your angel at a hotel is unusual, but if you were asked the question, 'Where do you suppose the most likely place would be to meet your guardian angel?' what would your answer be? A place of worship perhaps, or some remote countryside of outstanding beauty. I can guarantee no one would answer 'a typical English pub'! In fact this is exactly where Corrine met her angel.

It had been arranged that Corrine would meet her girlfriend after work for a drink. As the girlfriend was not known for her timekeeping, Corrine was not at all surprised to find herself waiting alone. She decided to go inside the pub and order a drink whilst she waited. On reflection she thought it had perhaps not been the wisest course of action because she was feeling very low and sitting alone in a near-empty pub made her feel isolated and vulnerable. Time passed and Corrine, sitting pondering her problems, began to feel depressed. Involuntarily, tears slipped down her cheeks and she was thankful that the pub was empty. Through the tears she became aware of a young man standing over her. Very distinctive in appearance, taller than average with very long dark hair, he was decidedly different in a way that Corrine could not quite grasp. Smiling kindly at her, he handed her a handful of blue paper napkins. 'You look as though you are in need of healing,' he said, 'so I have brought you some blue napkins, blue being the colour of healing.'

Accepting the napkins, Corrine dabbed her eyes. The young man sat beside her and introduced himself as the pub's new waiter. They started to chat and Corrine felt much calmer. He then said a surprising thing: 'Never forget that you are a diamond.' Corrine was slightly bemused. 'What do you mean?' she asked. His reply was equally confusing. 'Everyone in life has a specific purpose,' he answered. 'Your purpose is to be a diamond.'

At this point Corrine's friend arrived and joined them at the small table. Instantly she was distracted by another person and engaged in conversation. It was as though she was not intended to interrupt the important conversation taking place between Corrine and the young man. They were now discussing spiritual matters and a transformation was taking place in Corrine as they talked. Her worries and fears appeared to melt as she was overcome by a feeling of peace. Her life was suddenly crystal-clear, aspects that only moments ago had scared her now felt logical and she thought she could face them with serenity. Although a complete stranger, he knew all the answers to Corrine's problems and appeared to understand her life completely. The conversation drew to a close and he left the table.

Later that evening Corrine left with her friend and stood on the pavement as her friend was opening the car doors. Glancing back towards the pub Corrine saw the young man standing in the doorway. Repeating the message that she was a diamond, he turned and melted into the crowd. Corrine's friend said that she had had the distinct feeling she was being distracted to enable Corrine's conversation to continue, but had no idea why. It was all rather surreal, they concluded.

Inevitably Corrine's curiosity got the better of her and she returned to the pub. She was looking forward to chatting again to the remarkable young man. With disappointment she saw that he was not there. Enquiring at the bar when the new waiter would next be on duty, she was met with bewildered stares. 'What new waiter?' they asked. Corrine gave the description, saying that they must know him because he was so very distinctive in appearance. She was informed that it had been a long time since they had employed any new staff; their current employees had been a regular team for a long time. No one had ever seen a young man fitting Corrine's description.

Mulling all this over in her mind, Corrine is certain that this was no ordinary man. We discussed the symbolism of the message he had given her. Diamonds are symbols of purity and incorruptibility. More importantly they symbolise light. They are formed under intense pressure and emerge from the Stygian darkness of coal to the wonderful clarity of the gemstone. Corrine had indeed turned from darkness to light in that short space of time. Her life has continued purposefully from that day. The only conclusion she could possibly arrive at was that angels appear in the most unlikely places.

> 'We may not be aware of the presence of angels,
> We can't always predict how they will appear,
> But angels have been said to be our neighbours,
> Often they may be our companions without our being
> aware of their presence.'
>
> BILLY GRAHAM

I am often asked if I am aware of the 'parking angel'. Many people say that when urgently in need of a parking space, in some sort of an emergency, they ask their angel to help and amazingly a space appears. I have no evidence of this but one young lady felt she met an angel in a city parking lot one night.

A little nervously Amanda drove to the city. She had tickets for a pop concert but sadly at the last moment her friend had become ill and could not accompany her. Having looked forward to this occasion for a long time, Amanda was determined not to miss it. Parking her car in a city centre car park, amongst hundreds of others, she felt safe and was soon caught up in the excitement as she followed the crowds to the arena. The concert was every bit as good as she had hoped for and the audience was reluctant to let the band go. At last the end came and the crowds surged to exit from the huge arena. Amanda, slightly fearful of the crush and being at the very top of the building, decided to hold back a little whilst the crown thinned out. Stepping from the ladies' room some time later she realised to her surprise that it was half past midnight.

It was the city centre after all, she thought, and there will be many people about, no need to panic. However, on reaching the car park she was surprised to see it virtually empty. Hurrying to her car which was parked at the very back of the vast car park, she drove to the automatic barrier, realising that she was now the very last car to leave. Reaching into her handbag for the ticket to place in the barrier, she was distraught to discover that she had lost it! Fighting to control the rising panic, she slowly emptied the contents of her handbag onto the car seat; the ticket was definitely not there. She searched the car but it was nowhere to be found. Feverishly she wondered what on earth she could do. The barrier would not rise without the ticket, and she could not abandon her car and walk at this late hour through what was by now a deserted area.

The gravity of the situation was just sinking in when she was startled by a face appearing at the car window. She noticed with relief that the man was wearing a uniform – red cap and jacket – and was obviously a car park official. Winding down her window she was relieved to hear the man say, 'It is clear for you to drive on now,' and with that the barrier lifted. Thanking him profusely, she drove through and made her way home uttering a little prayer of thanks. Reaching home she realised that she was in fact shaking with shock. What on earth would I have done if that attendant hadn't still been around, she thought.

A few days later Amanda was in the city on a shopping trip and was passing the car park where she had been so frightened. She saw a young man taking motorists' money and issuing tickets. On impulse she decided to go and ask if the gentleman who had rescued her was on duty. The young man was confused by Amanda's description of the attendant. He was not young, she said, and had been wearing a red cap and coat. 'As you can see,' said the young man, 'our uniform is blue, a warm sweater and a blue baseball cap.' Amanda saw that this was in fact true. 'We do not have any elderly staff,' he continued. 'They are mostly students supplementing their grants.' Walking away, Amanda said to herself, 'It is clear to me that angels do not always dress in white and sport wings. Red cap or not, that was my angel.'

At times of bereavement or severe distress in our lives, we all find different ways to cope. It is true to say, however, that most people would feel better if they could talk about their feelings. Counselling is now an accepted form of help under such circumstances although a family member or close friend with a talent for listening is a real blessing. Men can often find unburdening themselves at such times extremely difficult. Frequently the 'stiff upper lip' takes over and feelings become bottled up.

Harry was no exception; the death of his wife had hit him hard and although he did long to talk about it, something inside held him back. Time passed and, as is often the case, physical problems developed with the stress of grief. Harry made an appointment at his doctors' surgery to seek help for several minor ailments.

Arriving at the surgery, he was told to see the doctor at the end of the corridor – she was free and would see him immediately. Sinking into the chair, Harry felt immediately at ease, despite the fact that the doctor was unfamiliar to him. The kind face with the welcoming smile and the deeply concerned expression in her eyes all made Harry relax. Sorting out his minor ailments quickly, she then said, 'There is something else we need to talk about, isn't there?' Harry said yes indeed, and found himself telling this young lady all about his wife and how much he missed her. Something had unlocked his tongue and out it all poured. After what must have been almost an hour, Harry thanked the doctor for taking the time to listen, assured her that he felt so much better, and, shaking hands, left. It was like a huge weight had been lifted from his shoulders and he arrived home with renewed confidence that he would in fact cope.

Three weeks later, a repeat appointment was required and once more Harry entered the health centre. He was told the name of the doctor he would be consulting. Telling the receptionist the name of the doctor he had seen previously he asked if he might have an appointment with her. 'We do not have a doctor of that name in this practice,' she replied. Harry assured her that it was in fact the name of the doctor he had seen and asked if it could have been a locum. 'No one has been away for months,' she said, 'and we certainly have not had a locum here in a long time!' To say Harry was bewildered would be an understatement, but he persisted and told the receptionist that he had definitely seen the lady. He gave a detailed description of her and declared that she had been in the consulting room with the blue door at the end of the corridor. Sighing loudly, the receptionist said that there had never been a doctor in the practice fitting the very distinctive description. The room with the blue door at the end of the corridor was not a consulting room, so he could not possibly have seen anyone in that room.

At this point Harry decided to keep quiet. He knew no matter what he said, he would not be believed. Formulating in his head was a theory. He had been very surprised that a normal appointment of only ten minutes had stretched into an hour or more. Such a long appointment was unheard of normally, he thought, and the lady had asked him what else he needed to talk about in a very knowing way. It was as if she knew he needed to unburden himself. No one had seen her before and they met in a room that was not ever used for consultations. Reflecting on the smile, the understanding eyes and the lovely feeling of peace he took away with him, he suddenly knew the answer. She had simply exchanged her white gown for a white coat, he concluded. And I for one agree.

✳ ✳ ✳ 5 ✳ ✳ ✳

Colour Surrounding Death

*'Colour is the keyboard, eyes are the hammers, the
soul is the piano with many strings.'*

WASSILY KANDINSKY

Colour is very important in all our lives. Psychologists discovered long ago how certain colours affect our wellbeing. Colour then affects all our lives, but what about our deaths? There is growing evidence that people in a near-death situation and even those who actually die will talk about colour. The colour most frequently described by those on the point of death is purple or lilac. There will often be an accompanying fragrance of the lilac flower or violets.

Eastern philosophy states that there are seven subtle energy centres within our bodies. These are known as 'the chakras'. Their colours, when visualised, help to balance our bodies and spirits, and they range from red through to violet. If we think about the chakras we will see that purple or violet colour relates to the crown and therefore the nearest point to heaven. Since ancient times purple has been the colour of the gods or signified the divine. Royalty, thought once to be divine, was always clothed in purple and it was only recently, historically speaking, that commoners were allowed to wear the colour. Symbolising heaven and spirituality, it is perhaps not a surprise then to find this colour associated with the end of our lives.

Martin was very close to death. He lay in the hospice bed holding his wife Margaret's hand in a very peaceful state. The staff had been wonderful, meeting his every need and making him very comfortable. It was clear to all that very soon he would simply slip away. Turning his head towards Margaret, he asked if there were any violets in the room – he could smell the wonderful scent, he said. His wife knew that there was only a vase of carnations which did not seem to have any fragrance whatsoever. He pointed towards the corner of the room. 'See,' he said, 'there they are, a huge display.' Margaret simply nodded although there were none to be seen. Minutes later he gently closed his eyes and died.

Knowing the end was near, Margaret was in many ways prepared, but it was not easy by any means to accept that Martin had finally gone. She closed her eyes and said a little prayer, asking that Martin would now be free and happy and requesting strength to help her carry on alone. Opening her eyes, she was met by the most astonishing sight. Martin was bathed in a wonderful purple light, surrounding him in the shape of an arc. The room filled with the most wonderful feeling of love and peace and, most powerfully, the scent of violets.

Picture the scene, Christmas 1998 and the pantomime season is in full swing. In the Cheshire town of Stockport, a Wednesday afternoon performance of Snow White is about to begin. Rows of excited children chattering in their seats, actors applying make-up and climbing into costumes. It is a familiar scene to many of us and conjures up many memories. However, it is the last possible setting one might imagine for a spiritual experience. In fact that is precisely what transpired.

Tony Monroe, an actor whose face will be familiar to many from his appearances on the small screen in popular programmes such as *EastEnders*, was sitting fully made up. He had a few moments before his call to the stage and he was quietly waiting. It was difficult for him to concentrate that afternoon. He was distracted by thoughts of his sister-in-law, who had died several days earlier. This afternoon was the time of her funeral and due to his theatrical commitments he was unable to attend. His thoughts were with the family and the emotional turmoil they would be facing. A deeply spiritual man, Tony was a healer and practised Reiki, an ancient form of Japanese healing. One form of helping people with this form of healing is to send, through meditation and thought, distant healing. It is common for most practitioners and certainly true of Tony, who would often send waves of healing to those in need.

The time of the funeral approached and Tony decided to concentrate and send his sister-in-law Reiki, enabling her to receive love as she moved into the next world. It was also Tony's way of saying goodbye as he could not be present. He decided to ask for a sign to indicate that his message had been received. This was something he occasionally requested and would feel a sensation of warmth in response. No response came on this occasion, so he sat simply thinking about his sister-in-law, looking through the open door of his dressing room and waiting for the call. Deep in contemplation, he sat sideways to the make-up mirror. Out of the corner of his eye he became aware of a bright light. His first reaction was that it was a reflection in the mirror. On close inspection he saw that the light was in fact hovering several inches in front of the mirror. It looked for all the world like a small stained-glass window. It was a wonderful deep cerise in colour and gave the impression of being several inches thick. Tony stared, mesmerised and mystified as to the nature of this wonderful light.

Eventually, after a minute or so, the light slowly started to move. It travelled all around the room, its brilliance never diminishing, until it reached the open door. It hovered for a minute or so in the doorway before moving into the corridor. The atmosphere radiating from the light was wonderful, an aura of peace hung in the air. Spellbound, Tony watched as the light slowly traversed the length of the corridor then gently faded away. Tony then realised with a jolt how amazing this was from another point of view. Normally at this point the corridor would be filled with actors and children waiting to go on stage. It was always a chaotic time and a last-minute panic about some detail or other was common, and yet here it was, the corridor leading directly to the stage, minutes before curtain up and all was quiet. Not a soul to be seen, and total silence backstage. Quite remarkable and unique in Tony's experience.

Later that evening he checked the sequence of events and times with his wife. It appeared that at the precise moment the wonderful light manifested in his dressing room, the funeral service had commenced. There seems to be no doubt that this was the response Tony had asked for. His sister-in-law was saying goodbye and confirming that healing and love transcend death itself.

I have often watched with amusement, and sometimes irritation, as people try to spell my name. The command 'name, please' is often followed by an eager beaver filling in the name before I have the chance to say, 'I shall have to spell that for you.' Frequently, after three or more attempts, they finally glance up and allow me to spell Glennyce for them. I have my Welsh-speaking grandfather to thank for the confusion. Ann, although Welsh-speaking, had a very simple name to spell. However, she never was called Ann, she tells me, unless she was in trouble – in fact her father called her Puff. As she grew up amongst her Welsh-speaking family she quickly learned to make herself scarce if anyone shouted 'Ann'. Despite this, Ann adored her father; he was, she says, a delightful character, very kind with a big heart. It was a close-knit family and when Ann lost both her parents within a few short months, she found it very difficult to bear.

When Christmas 2000 was celebrated, Ann could not believe it was four years since her parents had died. All the celebrations for the new millennium were in full swing and they would not be part of them. In the middle of all the excitement and bustle Ann started to feel unwell. By early January she was much worse and on calling the doctor to the house learned that she must go to hospital immediately. On arrival at hospital Ann was placed in the intensive care unit as she was by now slipping into a coma. The medical staff were most concerned and her chances of survival were not looking too promising. The coma deepened and she was to remain in that state for over twenty-four hours. Slowly she regained consciousness and everyone breathed a little easier. Although she was improving and was able to sit propped up in bed, Ann remained very poorly for some time. There was not at this time any medication administered, just watchful care.

Alone in the little room at this point Ann realised just how poorly she still was. Fear began to sweep over her and she found herself in tears. Then a wonderful arc of orange light radiated from one of her shoulders to the other. She felt completely enveloped in this warm, incredibly bright light and a sensation of comfort and love filled the whole room. Ann describes the feeling as being held in one's mother's arms when little and in distress. All her fear vanished and she had a sensation of being held by love.

Directly in front of Ann's line of vision, a tunnel appeared. It was dark and long and just at the very end she could see a bright light. Most amazing of all she then heard a voice speaking to her in Welsh. 'Go back, Puff,' it said, 'it is not yet your time, you have many happy years ahead with your husband.' It was without doubt her father's voice. Desperately Ann wanted to run to him and her mother; she felt all her strength draining away and knew she was on the brink of death. She found herself crying out for her parents, wanting to join them. The orange light intensified and seemed to hold her fast with a stronger feeling of comfort. It was at that moment the tunnel vanished, and she felt the life force returning. It was an amazing feeling to re-enter one's body, she says.

Ann had always believed in angels. When she was small her grandfather had told her about the Angel of Mons and how he had experienced their presence during the fierce battle of the Somme. It was now clear to her, on recovery, that the bright orange light was in fact angel wings embracing her. It was an act of guardianship, ensuring her recovery. It is a wonderful feeling to have known the angels were so near, Ann says with gratitude.

If the truth be told, Ruth was a little afraid of her grandmother. She was not a hard or cold person, but she was most definitely of the 'no-nonsense' school of grandparenting. Raised in a Victorian type of household, she found it difficult to unbend and show affection to her grandchildren. The fact that she loved them was nevertheless demonstrated in many ways.

Ruth discovered that when she left home to study at university, she missed her grandmother a great deal. On her visits home they were both especially pleased to be together again. Arriving home for the Christmas vacation during her second year of study, Ruth was upset to learn that her grandmother was very unwell. She deteriorated quickly and it was suggested that she be admitted to hospital. Strong to the last, she refused to go and so nursing care at home was arranged. Boxing Day morning arrived and Ruth's grandmother was fading fast. Ruth and her sister drove to their grandmother's house, discussing on the way how they felt about the prospect of losing her. They could not in all honesty describe their relationships as close but nevertheless they loved her and did not want to say goodbye.

A nurse greeted them on arrival and warned them that their grandmother had very little time left. Rushing upstairs to the bedroom they found her propped up amongst her pillows, very weak but clearly delighted to see them. Smiling, she held out a hand to each of them. Little was said but the girls told her that they loved her and were rewarded with the most wonderful smile and expression of peace on her face. Shortly after she died, Ruth caught a startled look on her sister's face but said nothing, deciding it must be the shock of seeing someone die. At this point their parents arrived and it was a highly emotional hour or so.

Some time later the sisters drove home, leaving their parents making arrangements from their grandmother's house. Making a cup of coffee, they sat down to discuss the events of the day. Ruth at this point decided to tell her sister just what had happened to her at the time of her grandmother's death. She had thought initially to keep the experience to herself but felt the need to talk about it. At the point of death, Ruth confided, she had seen a blue or lilac light radiate from behind their grandmother's bed. The air had filled with the scent of violets and she felt quite wonderful. Glancing towards her sister at that moment she had found her looking shocked and decided that she would not tell her what she had witnessed. To Ruth's surprise, her sister jumped from her chair and gave her an enormous hug. 'Thank goodness,' she said. 'I saw it too but thought I was hallucinating. The light and the accompanying fragrance startled me. I have never experienced anything similar before. I really thought it was all in my head, possibly due to the shock of Grandma dying.' Ruth realised why her sister had looked so shocked and wished she had said something at the time. However, it was quite wonderful to realise that angels were taking their grandmother to the next world and telling them with fragrance and colour that she loved them.

You will recall reading about Carol earlier in this book. Throughout her life she has felt very close to the spiritual world and acutely aware of messages at difficult times. From childhood, Carol had been close to her brother Stephen. He had always shown great support for his sister and always managed to make her laugh no matter how black things seemed. He had a wicked sense of humour and was a practical joker, definitely the live wire of the family. It was a sad day therefore for Carol when her brother Stephen went to live in South Africa. It did feel a very long way and she missed him a lot in spite of letters and phone calls. Stephen settled well to his new life and home. He married and had children, plus a successful career, which resulted in a very comfortable home and lifestyle. He loved music and was in demand as a disc jockey; life was sunny in every sense.

Sadly this sunny existence was not to last; his marriage failed. He worried terribly about the effect this would have on his children and it made him very sad. After his divorce he ploughed on, trying to do the best he could for his children. Six years had elapsed when suddenly life turned around for Stephen: he found himself in love. He was extremely happy with his new partner and Carol was delighted to hear the news, especially when they became engaged. The future looked very bright again. But Stephen, it seemed, was not destined to be happy for any length of time. His ex-wife was to prove very difficult about his new partner. Inexplicably she decided to make life as uncomfortable as possible for Stephen and his new partner. They came to the conclusion that because she had not found happiness elsewhere she found it hard to accept that Stephen had. The level of interference in the couple's lives became intolerable and inevitably took its toll on their relationship.

Stephen's new partner declared that although she loved him dearly, she could not tolerate the distress his ex-wife was causing. Sadly she left, and Stephen was distraught. All the fun and happiness in his life dissolved once more. His practical jokes and even his love of music suffered. Long telephone calls to Carol in England followed. There was little she could do except listen and hope that things would improve. The calls became more frequent and more desperate and one day Stephen told her that he was contemplating suicide. It was in the early hours of the morning and he had woken Carol from a deep sleep. It was difficult to absorb exactly what he was telling her and she did not think for one moment that he was serious. The following day, to Carol's deep distress, she received a call to tell her that the worst had in fact happened and Stephen was dead. What a terrible shock it was, and distressing to have been so far away and unable to help.

Arriving in South Africa for the funeral, Carol and her husband were met at the airport by Stephen's ex-fiancée. They instantly liked each other greatly and she drove them to Stephen's home where they were to stay during their time in the country. They chatted long into the night about Stephen, exchanging stories and even laughing about some of his jokes. Carol was told about his career as a DJ and how he had been particularly fond of green spotlights, always ensuring they surrounded him when he was playing his music. He even had them installed in his home, particularly the kitchen, which led to several jokes about the food looking slightly odd. The night before the funeral they retired to bed feeling very sad, not only because of the events of the forthcoming day but also that they had not met until this time. How Carol would have enjoyed getting to know this lovely young lady as her sister-in-law, had circumstances been different.

Sleep would not come that night and Carol sat up in bed thinking whilst her husband dozed beside her. She found herself fervently wishing that at last Stephen was at peace. To her amazement at this point something quite extraordinary happened. On the wall directly opposite the bed, a large circular green light appeared. Glowing brightly it was decidedly luminescent and pulsated in the dark. Stunned, Carol tried to think of explanations for this light. She got out of bed and opened the curtains, even though they were so thick the light could not have shone so clearly through them. Immediately outside the window was the pool, in complete darkness. There were no houses close enough to shed a light and in fact there was total darkness in every direction. Baffled, Carol woke her husband, and he declared it to be the moon. They went outside, but it was a moonless sky, only stars to be seen, and anyway, Carol pointed out, the moon is not green, even in Africa! It was obvious to Carol now that this was Stephen communicating and she gently spoke to the light, telling him that his partner of many years was in another room of the house. It had occurred to her that they were sleeping in the room Stephen and his ex-fiancée had once occupied. The light turned white and slowly faded. The whole episode had lasted about half an hour and all that time the light had remained bright green.

The following morning they discussed the night's events and Stephen's ex-fiancée was astonished, but agreed wholeheartedly that this was communication from

Stephen. His deep and unusual fascination with green spotlights was far too much of a coincidence. It was, they thought, his way of telling them that all was well, he was at last happy and at peace. Several incidents happened during the funeral which, amazingly, could only be described as amusing! The coffin would not go through the church door and had to be forced through a side door with difficulty. It then had to be manhandled over a piano, hardly gracious or reverent. Further amusing little things happened and Carol was forced to say that she felt Stephen would have found the whole thing very comical. They then all concluded that in fact it could well be Stephen's influence, continuing his practical joking. It certainly would be a way of assuring them that he was happy again.

In ancient times the rainbow was believed to be a bridge across which the soul travelled to heaven. A lovely image, it is true, but perhaps not just a lovely symbol, as our following story illustrates.

It was almost dark as Sheila started to prepare supper for her family. The day had been glorious and a wonderful sunset had kept Sheila and her family later than usual in the garden. The heady perfume of honeysuckle wafted through the kitchen window and all seemed right with the world. Just as the meal was served, however, Sheila received a phone call to say that her mother had been taken ill. Jumping into the car she rushed to her mother's home, mercifully only a few moments' drive away. An anxious neighbour greeted her and her mother's doctor was already in attendance. An ambulance had been called and Sheila held her mother's hand as they awaited its arrival. It appeared that the elderly lady had collapsed whilst gardening and suffered a heart attack. The neighbour had seen her fall and rushed to help. Thanking her kindly, Sheila promised to keep her informed of events as the ambulance pulled up outside the door. The neighbour left and the doctor went outside to meet the ambulance crew.

It was at that very moment that Sheila's mother died. It was unmistakable, momentarily her eyes opened and she faintly smiled at Sheila. 'It was as if I could actually see her soul departing,' Sheila said. 'Almost lovely, the sensation of peace filling the room.' To her utter astonishment there then appeared a huge rainbow of colour, encircling her mother's head. It was quite perfect in every detail, as if there had been rain and sun within the little room. The fact was that it was now dark outside and only a lamp lit the room. The doctor returned but, seeing Sheila's face and being only too familiar with the vital signs, he realised at once that his patient had died. 'Can you see anything?' Sheila asked. The doctor replied, 'Yes, all the signs are there. I am sorry to say we are too late to help your mother.' It was obvious that he could not see this wonderful rainbow and Sheila decided not to say anything about the experience.

It was a long time, she told me, before she shared this story with anyone. Deeply personal and very moving, she knows it was her own angel sign that her mother had gone across the bridge to heaven.

$* \text{\Large *} * 6 \text{\Large *} * *$

Visions

How does one define a vision? I have come to the conclusion that it is easier to say what it definitely is not rather than what it actually is. During the course of writing this book I spoke to Maggie Harrison. She is the patient support officer at Henshaw's Society for the Blind. We had a fascinating talk about hallucinations, a condition sadly affecting many people as they suffer gradual blindness. This condition is called Charles Bonnet Syndrome. He discovered that when someone's eyesight fails and the visual image decreases, the brain takes over. It substitutes an image from memory or the imagination. The images are vivid and exact, often frightening, or at the very least worrying. Maggie said, 'In simple terms, eyes do little more than convert light energy into electrical energy in the form of "nerve pulses". Specific patterns of nerve impulses are generated according to the nature of light falling on the retina. These images are transmitted to the visual cortex of the brain, where they are further processed to access other areas of the brain.' The frightening condition of Charles Bonnet Syndrome has been recognised since 1760 when discovered by the Swiss philosopher Bonnet, and has produced scenes of huge forests suddenly appearing, images of men throwing knives, monsters emerging from ordinary faces. Truly dreadful experiences.

Compare this with the visions related to me. People relate overwhelming feelings of love and peace, visions of angels distinctly different from any paintings one might have seen, colours of hues not seen on earth and scenes that could never have been in a person's memory. Visions often appear when people most need comfort, help or guidance and appear only once. Frequently they can occur when a spiritual atmosphere is present, endorsing the 'other world' content. They are usually life-changing and affirming, wonderful events which leave a permanent, positive memory. No fear and certainly no worry is associated with these visions, the incident completely eliminates any worry or distress the person previously felt. Judge for yourself how wonderful and uplifting visions can be, as you contemplate Ruth's experience.

> 'The garments of the angels correspond to their
> intelligence. The garments of some glitter as with
> flame and those of others are resplendent as
> with light. Others are various colours,
> and some white and opaque.'
>
> EMANUEL SWEDENBORG

I am frequently asked, 'How do I get in touch with the angels?' and I always answer that if you are 'open' and you need them they will find you. Many people who are not in need, facing danger or distressed also have angelic encounters. It may be that they are at that moment so spiritually aware and in tune that the angels can come through. I certainly believe this was the case for Ruth, who was blessed with a very special angel encounter.

Many of you reading this book will be familiar with the writings of Eileen Elias Freeman. Inspiring to read and certainly to hear speak, she attends many angel days and seminars. A special angel day was held at the Bryn Athyn Cathedral in Philadelphia and Eileen was the guest speaker. The cathedral was packed for this very special day. Ruth was soaking up the atmosphere as she waited for Eileen to arrive on the platform. The sense that this was going to be a unique experience was plain from the very beginning. Eileen began by asking everyone to bow their heads in prayer. Ruth closed her eyes, feeling empathy with the prayer, and it was at this point that the most remarkable vision occurred.

She had stepped into an angel 'scene', its loveliness taking her breath away. Here are Ruth's own words as she describes it: 'I was standing behind a row of angels; they were each arrayed in gowns of luxuriant hue. The colours ranged from jewel-box tones to sunset rays. I was behind one particular angel robed in a light turquoise and if I moved my head I could see way beyond her.' The angels then started to move, reaching out their hands to clasp the hand of the angel on either side. As Eileen's voice could be heard speaking the prayer the host of angels bowed their heads in unison, joining the prayer. Ruth says she had the distinct feeling that they had assembled to wait for the prayer. The story continues in Ruth's words: 'At first I thought the angels formed a circle, but I was able to step back and then realised that it was in fact a huge unbroken spiral.' Nearest to Ruth was the angel wearing the deepest jewel-coloured robes. And Ruth is adamant that they had wings. Continuing down the spiral the robes became of more muted colours and hues. At the lowest point of all the angels appeared to be in dress of human type.

Awe-struck, Ruth tried to take all this in but then realised that in fact the spiral continued upwards also. She describes what she saw gazing up: 'Above the jewel-coloured angels was another row of amazing beings. This time the robes were without colour but of luminous, iridescent white. Their bodies seemed indistinguishable from their robes and they radiated light.' Observing that these angels were much larger than the others, she says they stood tightly packed shoulder to shoulder in shimmering rows.

To Ruth's amazement she was able to move backwards and forwards in this scene to be able to view the whole panorama. The wonderful spiral was shrouded in pale white mist and descended as far as she could see. Love and energy appeared to emanate from this mist which was at its most intense around the higher spiral of angels. At no time did this obscure Ruth's view and amazingly throughout this time Ruth could clearly hear Eileen's voice and her words of prayer. The angels were in harmony with this prayer, affirming with an almost humming noise echoing up and down the spiral. It is an experience Ruth will never forget;

a deeply meaningful day when the angels joined everyone in Bryn Athyn Cathedral.

The deeper I delve into people's experiences with the angelic world, the more astounded I am by the myriad ways in which they manifest themselves. I long ago came to the conclusion that we receive what we can cope with. A gentle hand on the shoulder, a fragrance, or a voice may be enough to reassure most of us. Other encounters are more dramatic and are experienced by those who perhaps need them most. Different people see widely differing shapes and forms, yet each person is always clear in his or her own mind that what occurred was of an angelic nature. The common denominator and the deciding factor would seem to be the overwhelming feelings of love and peace. Hearing John's story, one would not immediately think of angels. No doubt exists in John's mind, however, that even though the form was not of an easily identifiable nature, the contact he experienced was angelic.

John tells a story that is not only most unusual, it is also very moving and uplifting. I will let him explain in his own words exactly what occurred after the death of his wife. 'Deanna had been ill for two years, a time which proved to have happiness mingled with the pain. One Saturday morning, in a Bournmouth hospital, my beloved wife passed away. The overwhelming feeling for me was the knowledge that she was now at peace, all suffering ceased. A day of confusion and mixed emotions followed. So many arrangements to be made, so many people to contact. It was not until 10.30 pm that night that I found myself alone at last. Climbing into bed, with just a small bedside light for illumination, I pondered the day's events.'

John continues: 'Lying back I instantly felt a great wave of peacefulness envelop me, I was totally calm. In front of my eyes there then appeared several golden specks of light. These travelled towards me, increasing in number, until eventually my entire field of vision was filled with them. Growing in size, they became large, beautiful orbs of golden light, shimmering and literally splashing against my eyes. I began to accept the phenomenon and became totally absorbed in the beauty of the event. There was by now a multitude of lights, merging and changing into a huge golden aura. Suddenly within this aura of light, a single grey shape emerged and disappeared. This was repeated with ever-increasing numbers of grey shapes, vibrating against the now still backdrop of gold light. The shapes were featureless, but strangely I instinctively knew them to be my family and close relatives who had previously died. They radiated waves of pure love.'

For some time this amazing event continued, and John felt as though the heavenly host itself was involved. Eventually there emerged one huge grey mass that seemed to engulf all the shapes into its form. It vibrated and gave John the impression of a huge life force. All this time, he says, the bedroom was clearly visible; he was able to identify the ceiling, walls and curtains clearly. By his side the single bedside light glowed dimly, and, thinking quite rationally, John mused on the fact that this extraordinary event was happening in the most ordinary of settings.

The vision began to change, the light became still and the background a dark blue. A brilliant blue flashing light, similar to lightning, crossed John's field of vision. Slabs of blue light followed, morphing into shapes of many differing colours. Beautiful and iridescent, the shapes flowed in a continuous stream before John's eyes. He actually felt his eyes and head begin to ache at this point, but was filled with the wonder of it all. White light followed in arcs, leaving trails behind them reminiscent of comets. Could this, John thought, be the Holy Spirit? Certainly those were the words resounding in his head. Slowly it all began to fade until the last shape and colour had disappeared. He was left with the sensation that somehow he had been privileged to witness a glimpse of eternal life.

One would think that this amazing and stimulating vision would have left a person in a state of great agitation. The last thing possible would be sleep. Incredibly John had the sensation of being gently laid down in his bed, and instantly he fell asleep. The following morning, John was delighted to receive a visit from Deanna's surgeon. He had become a friend over the years and kindly called to see how John was coping. He listened intently to John's story of the night before and was visibly moved, replying that he was convinced that the bereaved are sometimes given these wonderful insights. Always a believer in God and the afterlife, this experience confirmed John's beliefs. It certainly helped him through his grief and sadness. He realised also what a precious gift life was and that we should live it to the full. The most wonderful aspect of that night, the amazing feelings of love coming unannounced but when he needed them most, has stayed with him to the present day.

It was April and the early morning sun held no warmth. The North Sea rolled onto the beach and crashed at Vicky's feet. Skilfully dodging the waves and occasionally skimming pebbles, she was deep in thought. Life for Vicky was at a crossroads and she had to make a momentous decision. Promotion in her chosen career would involve moving away to a location at the other end of the country. Family and friends would all be left behind and yet she felt that possibly the time had come for her to be brave. The deserted beach calmed her a little but she also realised just how much she would miss it.

Sitting on a boulder, she turned the collar of her coat up against the wind and reflected on the fact that she could use some tangible sign to guide her. She silently said a little prayer asking for help. A sensation of warmth engulfed her and a vista of golden light opened in front of her. In the centre of this light a figure slowly emerged. The figure was dressed in shimmering blue and both arms were extended towards Vicky. She felt no fear, even though she could not see the face of this figure, enclosed as it was by a large hood. Happiness and love flowed from this vision and a peace that calmed Vicky as never before. The light changed from a gold shade to a deep pink and all this was accompanied by a sweet musical sound. She could still see the waves and the beach and was aware of the birds flying past. In the blink of an eye it was gone and she found herself sitting once more on the boulder alone with the sea. It was now once more bitingly cold, the wonderful warm sensations had completely gone. Vicky made her way home along the beach. This time there was no doubt in her mind as to her future path. Instinctively she knew that no matter where she went care and protection would surround her. Fear melted away, the decision was clear and easy to make. 'I think I just met my very own "angel of the north",' she said.

We have discussed how difficult it is to say exactly what constitutes a vision; it is certainly not a dream, but one has a distinct feeling of being out of the normal waking state. Sometimes people are aware of their surroundings, whilst at the same time being transported to a different plane. I found our next story fascinating, especially so since John's account had very similar elements. Both describe angels as grey shapes, a rare description but obviously not unique. Circumstances were very different despite the fact that both were receiving help. Catherine is a very conscientious, down-to-earth teacher, active in local politics, and has a busy social life. She is not at all fanciful, but like most of us is subject to times in her life when she feels rather low. Her story begins on a day that would make anyone feel down.

The day was decidedly grey, clouds of pewter sailing menacingly overhead. A light drizzle hung in the air rather than fell and it was clear that the day was not going to improve. In truth the weather matched Catherine's mood – no sign of blue skies in any sense. She was fully conscious of the fact that she was working too hard, denying herself treats or even moments of relaxation. Nevertheless she ploughed on despite the notion at the back of her mind that if she did not slow down she would most definitely be ill. At last she decided to give herself a treat and that for Catherine meant a lovely aromatic massage. Aware of the fact that her muscles were tense, she knew this to be a form of relaxation that had worked in the past. It would soothe the spirit as well as the body. The appointment was made and that simple act in itself cheered her slightly.

Driving through the mist was far from pleasant and it was with a sigh of relief that Catherine pulled up on to the drive of her friendly masseuse's house. Before long she was lying on the comfortable table, breathing in the wonderful fragrant oils and relaxing under the smooth hands of the professional. Tension drained away and the knots of muscles began to unravel. It was the practice of Catherine's masseuse to work on one part of the body and then pause for some deep breathing before moving on. As she lay listening to this deep breathing Catherine found herself thinking just how vulnerable and in need of support she felt. If only new life could be breathed into her, she thought, and help renew her energy levels. She pondered that she did not know where the help or support might come from. True, she was blessed with loving parents and lots of loyal friends, but her inner feelings and worries were most difficult to share. There was always the reluctance to burden or worry them.

By this point the lady was working on her feet and the symbolism of standing alone occurred to Catherine and again the overpowering sensation of needing support engulfed her. It was then that it happened, the most astonishing experience of Catherine's life. She felt warm, dry hands slip underneath her body and she was transported to another place. Here she was surrounded by thousands of beings, all dressed in pale grey. The garments were chador-like, pale in shade and covered the beings from head to toe. They gave the appearance of being almost triangular in shape and Catherine knew instinctively that they were all female. Intense feelings of love and support surrounded her. Gazing around, Catherine was aware of being in an extremely large building reminiscent of an aircraft hangar. The whole of this huge space was filled by the grey figures and Catherine's instinctive feeling was of an angel host. Soft voices spoke to her and she realised with amazement that the voices of the figures far away in the building could be heard as clearly as those of the figures standing next to her. All the communication was of love and support and the emphatic sensation that she was not, nor ever would be, alone. The vision was quite wonderful and seemed to last for hours. Gently, this fantastic scene faded away and Catherine found herself back in the little room. It was with sheer incredulity that Catherine then realised that this whole episode had taken place during the time it had taken her masseuse to take three deep breaths.

It has been five years since this awesome experience and for a long time after that day Catherine had the sensation of those supporting hands on her back. Should she feel the need to be reassured at any time, she concentrates and the feeling of love and support returns. It seems to be that the symbolism of the aircraft hangar and its implications of flight were to release Catherine's feelings of being bogged down. The thousands of angels were clearly supporting Catherine, assuring her she would never be alone. This was a unique and wonderful vision delivering a powerful message.

It is true to say the sun was beating down fiercely; this was after all the Indian Ocean. James was on board a troop ship bound for Singapore. It was 1948 but James recalls the occasion as if it happened yesterday, so clearly has it remained in his mind. Serving as a National Serviceman he found differing emotions mixed together. On the one hand he found the excitement of seeing faraway places quite wonderful but at the same time he suffered pangs of home-sickness. He missed his family, and his girlfriend. At home in London, James's mother was feeling emotional too, worrying as all mothers would at having her young son so far away.

James had been working hard all day, moving heavy crates around the ship and when he at last had a break he found the heat and the effects of the exertion made him feel quite exhausted. He stretched out on deck to relax, thinking of home and particularly of his girlfriend and mother. A strange sensation overcame him, one he struggles to describe as it was unlike anything he had ever encountered before. He had the sensation of descending into a familiar street in London. It was as if he was in a trance and most definitely not asleep. He recalls virtually floating down the main thoroughfare of the area where he lived, until he approached the side road where his house was. Stopping at his front door he knocked upon it firmly.

James had the feeling of returning to reality and became aware of the ship moving gently beneath him. How strange it all felt – he was not at all sleepy, he just had an unworldly sensation. Glancing at his watch he saw that it was 5 pm, eight hours ahead of London time, and he wondered what everybody was doing at home. Several days later the shipped docked at Changi, Singapore, where to everyone's delight there were huge sacks of mail awaiting them. A letter for James from his mother contained fascinating news. She wrote to say that early one morning she had heard a knock on the front door. She felt instinctively that it was James. She rushed to open the door, wondering if he had unexpectedly been granted home leave. However, on opening the door she discovered no one there. With a jolt she realised that it could not possibly have been James – after all, he was half a world away. She had nevertheless heard a distinct knocking and was baffled to find the street completely empty. It was of course exactly the same time James had had his strange experience. They discussed these events when James eventually came home. It was obvious to them that James had made his presence felt to his mother at a time when she was particularly worried about his safety and wellbeing. We all possess an 'angel within', and James's story illustrates the spiritual connecting of such 'inner angels'.

✳ ✳ ✳ 7 ✳ ✳ ✳

Aromatic Angels

*'The garland combines the symbolism of the flower
and the ring. It also stands for the binding together of
this world and the next.'*

DAVID FONTANA

The circle representing eternity has since ancient times been woven with flowers, and today it is still evident in the funeral wreath. The scent of the flowers represents the fragrance of heaven. Our first story tells of fragrance from medieval times reaching out in a very significant way across the centuries.

Summer sliding into autumn is often the most glorious time of the year; warmth without burning heat, colours of nature mellowing to match one's mood. The hint of harvest and misty mornings gladden the heart. Such days are perfect for walking in the countryside, soaking up the beauty and enjoying the fresh air. Leaning on a gate with a panoramic view of the Yorkshire Dales seemed a wonderful idea. Audrey and her husband persuaded a couple of friends to join them and off they set on a glorious autumn day. It was truly England's green and pleasant land that day and the friends happily explored Wensleydale in perfect weather conditions. Reaching a place called West Witton, they were intrigued to find some very interesting ruins. From the shape and form of the ruins it had clearly been a place of worship. It had in fact belonged to the Knights Templar and several areas were still intact. There was a clearly identifiable stone altar and behind this altar they discovered two stone coffin shapes. They were small in length and the friends discussed how it seemed that the occupants had not been very tall. After some time the group decided to continue on their way.

Audrey lingered behind, intrigued by the stone coffin shapes. The group were out of sight and Audrey decided to lie down in one stone indentation to see just how long they were. Being tiny herself, she was delighted to find that she in fact fitted the shape exactly. Somehow this was strangely fascinating to her and she felt a lovely atmosphere in that sacred place as she gazed up at the deep blue sky. The history of the place filled her with awe. She thought of all the souls who had worshipped and died in this place. It did in fact date from the thirteenth century. However, Audrey was totally unprepared for the events that followed. Softly, the most wonderful music swelled around her, quite unlike any she had ever heard. 'No words could describe it,' she says. 'I am at a loss when I try.' Simultaneously she was engulfed by the most incredible fragrance. The combination of the music and the fragrance filled her with wonder and there was no doubt that they emanated from the stone beneath her. Her heart felt full; it was a special moment and she was relieved that the other members of her group had gone on ahead. It was an experience for her alone and she felt both blessed and privileged. Rising to her feet she glanced around. All was stone or grass, no flowers to be seen, although she could not imagine any earthly flower producing such a fragrance. She knew inside that the sensations revealed to her were not of this world and that on that day she had received a gift to be cherished.

The relationship between granddaughter and grandmother is often quite unique, each bringing their special attributes to the bond. Wisdom and caring which come with age, wonder and innocence from the young. This frequently produces a spontaneous love, which grows with the years. Deborah had just such a bond with her grandmother, enjoying a lovely relationship as she grew up.

On reaching adulthood Deborah became a qualified nurse, so it was with great concern and insight that she heard of her grandmother's illness. Cancer had been diagnosed, and it was of little surprise to the family that she chose to confide her innermost feelings to her granddaughter. Deborah was there for her whenever she needed to talk, and this was especially appreciated as it had been many years since her husband had died. Facing her illness bravely, she told Deborah that she had always had a strong belief in life after death and that death was not something to be afraid of.

Eventually, Deborah's grandmother had to move to a hospice to spend her last few days, and she was made extremely comfortable. Her family was very supportive and she was never alone in the pretty little room. The day arrived when it was obvious that little time was left; the old lady had been slipping in and out of a coma for most of the morning. They had discussed how Deborah's grandparents had met, laughing about how Grandfather had agreed to take her swimming. He knew that she was a strong, keen swimmer, and in his eagerness to take her out he failed to mention that in fact he was a non-swimmer! Rashly he had promised a day out at the beach and a swim in the sea. It had been a source of great amusement ever since, although Grandma did teach him to swim. The sea was very dear to them both and had special meaning for them.

At this moment Deborah was surprised to see a bright, white light pierce the dull day and shine through the window directly upon her grandmother. It was quite unlike any light she had ever witnessed before. Stronger and far brighter than sunbeams it rested on her grandmother's face as accurately as a spotlight. To add to this amazing event, and most poignant of all, the air was suddenly filled with the smell of the sea. It was powerful and unmistakeable. The message was unmistakeable also; Grandfather had come to take his much loved wife to heaven. Looking at her grandmother Deborah realised that she had in fact just died, but had the most wonderful expression on her face of happiness and peace.

It was indeed a most moving experience, but the story contains one more intriguing element. Deborah's father had that morning gone into town on business. He was to join them at the hospice as soon as possible. Completing his business he glanced up at the clock in the tower of the town's guildhall and noticed it was 2.30 pm. Checking to see if his own wristwatch was accurate, he was pleased to see that it also registered 2.30 pm. Some time later he arrived at the hospice to be told that Grandma had died at precisely 2.30 pm. Surprised, he automatically looked at his wristwatch; it had stopped at exactly that time.

Anthony expected his bride to look beautiful, but when he saw Sian walking down the aisle, he says, he thought she looked like an angel. How lovely she looked; in fact everything was lovely, the tiny flower-filled church and the faces of all the guests. Anthony's grandmother beamed in her huge pink hat, frail at the age of ninety but enjoying herself immensely. The sight of the young bridesmaid with her shining face reminded Anthony that this was a day to be enjoyed by all. Not for the first time that day Anthony wished that his mother could have been with them. Sadly she had died three years previously, and was missed greatly by all the family. How she would have loved today, he thought, and felt his eyes prick with tears.

The service went smoothly and soon Anthony and Sian followed the vicar into the vestry to sign the register. There was in the little room, Anthony thought, the most amazing fragrance and he asked Sian if she could smell the lovely scent. Looking at him quizzically, she answered, 'It is my flowers.' Bending across Sian to sign the register, Anthony noticed that the bridal bouquet had a very different fragrance from the strong, heady one he was aware of. An hour of having photographs taken and fun on the church lawn was followed by a jolly ride to the country restaurant where the reception was to be held.

More photographs were taken here in the stunning gardens and the sun shone on cue to make everything perfect. A waiter approached Anthony – could he spare a moment to have a quick word with the manager, there had been a minor hitch. Anthony followed him into the dining room and was relieved to hear that it was indeed only a minor problem and it was quickly sorted out. Turning, he left the dining room by another exit and found himself in a large glass conservatory. Through the patio doors was a wonderful view of the surrounding countryside. Pausing a moment to take in the view, Anthony was suddenly once more surrounded by the same strong, most unusual fragrance. It had appeared as if from nowhere. Glancing around he noticed that although the conservatory was filled with ferns there were no flowers of any kind. This time there was no doubt in Anthony's mind; a real angel was with him now, his mother had not missed his special day after all.

We are aware of the dangers associated with smoking. Thousands try to give up the habit and not all of them succeed. Alice was one who, having tried to stop time and time again, decided to give up trying and simply carry on smoking. Her friends decided not to nag and simply accepted her decision, although they did worry about her health. It was obvious to all when Alice was present because she smoked the very distinctive Gauloise brand, with its strong odour. It gave her a Continental air, Alice said, much to her friends' amusement. At the age of fifty, Alice suffered a heart attack and the road to recovery proved to be a long one. Living alone, she was grateful for her close and loyal friends. A rota was organised to attend to her needs. Alice pondered on the saying that in time of need you discover your true friends. How fortunate she was to have a group so willing to help her. Barbara had been a close friend since childhood and Alice had always been included in Barbara's family. Holidays and special occasions were spent in Barbara's house and she was an honorary aunt to Barbara's children.

Three months later Alice appeared to be recovering well. She was her old cheerful self again and persuaded her friends to join her on her new gentle exercise regime. They took walks and swimming sessions together, which proved to be most pleasurable and beneficial to everyone. The shock, therefore, when Alice was found dead in her easy chair one morning, was considerable. It was difficult to absorb and everyone was most distressed, especially Barbara. After the funeral, Barbara had to arrange for the sale of the house and contents, Alice having had no close relatives. It was a dreadful task. Barbara was overcome with the feeling that Alice might feel alone and worried constantly about this. Having spent so many years looking out for her friend in this life, she found herself worrying about her in the next. Friends and family laughed at Barbara and her husband said, 'I thought you believed in angels. Surely they are taking care of Alice now.' Suddenly the room filled with the unmistakeable smell of Gauloise tobacco smoke. No other smoker in the house, there was only one possible explanation. Alice was telling them that she was definitely being looked after by the angels!

Some people believe in angels, some people see angels and some people simply are angels! Valerie, I am quite sure, is one of these. Albeit a down-to-earth, very practical angel. With a medical background, Valerie is a professional first aid trainer. Her first love is an angelic calling; working hard, she finances her own trips to India to work with the street children of Bombay. She takes medical skills and love in abundance to all who need her. Many amazing stories surround these visits; often when she is at her wits' end wondering where the medical equipment or finances will come from, the very item or amount of money will appear out of the blue. Her life is a testament to angelic synchronicity, enabling her to continue her valuable work.

At the age of sixteen, Valerie became all too aware of the power of angels. Her story is one of inspiration. She found herself one day in the most excruciating pain and began praying for help. She had a mischievous personality and she found herself promising God that if she received help she would be good! Valerie's mother was a hospital matron and on arriving home was confused not to see her daughter preparing the evening meal as usual. Climbing the stairs she was horrified to find Valerie clutching her abdomen in pain. Her father had arrived home shortly before and was relieved to see his wife, knowing her expertise in the field. In no time at all Valerie was in a speeding ambulance on her way to hospital. She recalls seeing the reflection of the blue flashing light in the store windows as they sped past. The knowledge that she would soon be at the hospital kept her going despite that terrible pain.

Hands lifted her on to a trolley and she was rushed along the corridor towards the operating theatre. She was aware of the blur of light overhead passing at speed, green masked faces and, finally, merciful oblivion. Peritonitis had been the cause of so much pain, and the operation was not a moment too soon, for the ruptured appendix had made her life hang in the balance for a while. A soft Irish voice whispered, 'She is sleeping, that's good,' and Valerie was aware of a cool hand on her brow. The pain went and was replaced by a lovely floating feeling. Oblivious to her surroundings she drifted in and out of consciousness. Every time she woke there was the most wonderful smell of lavender, gentle and soothing, even promoting a feeling of healing.

Eventually the voice and the fragrance materialised as a person. Valerie was awake and aware that the most beautiful lady was sitting by her bed. 'Hello, Valerie,' the lady said. 'How are you, dear?' It was not a dream, of that Valerie is certain, even thought at this point she was a little disoriented. She realised that the sweet fragrance of lavender was emanating from this lady, who gently held her hand. Whenever Valerie woke from sleep, there she was, gently smiling and comforting. Valerie thought of her as 'my lavender lady', concluding that she must be a hospital visitor. Slowly Valerie became more aware of her surroundings and began to notice details of her lady visitor. She wore a brown calf-length skirt and highly polished ankle boots with silky stockings in between. Her blouse was extremely dainty, cream in colour with a delicate lace collar. Most attractive of all, for Valerie, were the tiny pearl buttons which fastened this delightful blouse. Her hair was a deep chestnut colour, thick and wavy, tucked behind one ear. The other ear, Valerie noticed, had a long drop pearl earring clipped to it.

Still very poorly although improving slowly, she listened as the lady sang to her, stroked her hair and told her forcibly that she must not die because it was not her time. As she stroked Valerie's hair it was as if energy was flowing into her and she had the sensation that the lady was essential to her recovery. The vigil at the bedside was constant; the lady did not appear to go home with the other visitors and one fact confused Valerie. All the other visitors were dressed in light summer clothing and Valerie wondered why her lady dressed so inappropriately, if smartly. None of this mattered, however; she felt herself improve and that was a wonderful sensation.

Eventually her recovery was sufficient for the doctors to transfer her to a local cottage hospital for recuperation. She could regain her strength gradually and it felt good to be sitting up surrounded by her family. Sadly for Valerie the lady had gone, but Valerie reasoned that she was attached to the main hospital as a volunteer. She did ask her family at this point why none of them had visited her whilst she was in the big hospital. Astonished, the family told her that they had been with her around the clock, because she had been so poorly. At various points they feared that they would lose her. They had all been very distressed and spent a good deal of the time weeping. No one mentioned the lavender lady, which confused Valerie considerably, and she decided to remain silent about her for the time being.

Home at last they all chatted about the drama and Valerie decided that perhaps now she would tell them about the extraordinary hospital visitor. Her brothers and sisters along with her parents sat listening intently to her story. She described the lady in detail, her clothing and so on and of course her wonderful scent. At this point, to everyone's astonishment, Valerie's mother fainted. Everyone ran to her aid, and when she had recovered sufficiently, Valerie's father went upstairs and returned with a small box. It was a little locked chest that no one had seen before. 'Look at this, darling,' her mother said. The casket contained small treasures belonging to Valerie's grandmother. She had died when Valerie's mother had been a young girl of thirteen and the box had been stored away in the attic for many years.

At the bottom of the small treasure chest lay a sepia photograph and it was handed to Valerie. There smiling up at her was the lavender lady! Perfect in every detail – clothes, hair and even the drop pearl earring in one ear. The entire family were at first speechless, then Valerie's mother added that this lovely lady had always kept a small pad of cotton wool soaked in lavender oil next to her skin.

It was the grandmother Valerie had never seen, and this was the only photograph in existence as far as Valerie's mum knew, which was why it had been stored away for safekeeping. Rarely had Valerie's mother spoken about her, for the memory of losing her at such a tender age was still painful, and certainly Valerie had never heard a description of how she had looked.

Something incredible and very special had occurred. The family became overcome with emotion, hugging each other at a loss for words. The lavender lady was in fact the lavender grandmother, appearing in Valerie's hour of need to save her and return her to her anxious family. Valerie says that she is very fortunate to know the identity of her guardian angel and never ceases to wonder at her timely intervention.

✶ ✳ ✳ 8 ✳ ✳ ✶

Near-death Experiences

'We cannot fully understand this life, until we catch a glimpse of what lies beyond.'

RAYMOND MOODY

Carl Jung, the famous Swiss psychologist, always called death 'the great adventure'. He believed that what came after death was 'unspeakably glorious'. He formed this opinion after an amazing near-death experience. He suffered a heart attack at the age of sixty-nine. Typical sensations of leaving his body were followed by looking down on the Earth from space. He tells us Earth was bathed in a beautiful blue light and he could see distinctly each continent. His description of the Earth from space was amazingly accurate and this was long before space travel. After the experience Jung's nurse told him that she had been convinced he was dying as there was a golden, other-worldly glow surrounding him that she had only witnessed before around patients who died.

'Small are we, and small our planet
Hidden here among the stars,

May we know our timeless mission,
Universal atavars.'

RODGER TAYLOR WALKE

The light people refer to in near-death experiences is often labelled 'the being of light'. This is thought to be a spiritual being awaiting our journey to the next world and helping us transcend from our earthly plain to the higher one. Virtually all near-death experiences tell of this amazing light. The collection of stories in this chapter are no exception.

When Rod wrote to me his letter began, 'I will never forget the day I died.' Not too many people would be able to say that! A pastor at the Emmanuel Church in Brentwood, Staffordshire, Rod leads a very busy life. His story begins on a very cold February day in 1985. The snow was falling and had built up during the night, blocking the path to Rod's house. The family was all at home – Pauline, Rod's wife, and their two daughters Susan and Sarah. All were surprised at the depth of the snow and Rod decided there was nothing for it but to get his large shovel from the garage and set to work. Vigorously he started to clear the snow, keeping up quite a pace. Without warning, Rod suddenly felt a sharp pain in his chest, so severe it made him yell. The shock was great and he called urgently for help. Pauline and his daughter Susan, then aged fourteen, rushed to his aid. Together they managed to drag Rod, not a small man by any means, into the house.

Pauline attempted to make him comfortable and it went through her mind that he might have suffered a stroke.

Leaving Susan momentarily, she dashed to their neighbour's house for help. It was at this point that Rod literally died. His poor distraught daughter saw this was the case, realising instantly that her father was dead. She became hysterical at the sight of her dear father, who had changed colour, completely stopped breathing and was almost rigid. All she could do was wait for help but she already knew it was too late.

We now see the situation from Rod's perspective, quite literally the story from the other side. Whilst his family tried to help him, he recalls the sensation of leaving his body at speed. This speed increased as he found himself travelling down a dark tunnel. The severe pain had gone and he experienced a heightening of all his natural senses. Hearing was astonishingly acute, colours amazingly vivid. As a Christian, Rod was aware of what was happening, especially when he saw at the end of the tunnel an incredibly white light. It was brilliant yet gentle and was pulling him as if by a magnet to its very centre. He believed that he was about to enter heaven. The tunnel was coming to an end and the light increasing and he felt the radiance about to engulf him. At this point he recalls the name 'Jesus' being spoken very loudly. Three times a voice shouted the name and it resulted in what Rod can only describe as an emergency stop! He had the distinct sensation of reversing, travelling once more at incredible speed through the tunnel. He realised that he was entering his body and became aware that the voice he could hear was that of his wife. She had called out to Jesus asking him to save her husband.

Opening his eyes, Rod was now aware that he was clearly back home, surrounded by his family and neighbours, their fearful faces covered with tears. Soon he was admitted to hospital for tests. His arteries were completely furred up and he was warned that he was seriously ill. Rod had a trip planned to the USA in the very near future as part of his ministry. The doctor told him that there was no way he could make the trip. Days later, when the medical tests were completed, to everyone's astonishment they came back negative. Rod was cleared to travel and did indeed visit America just one week later.

As a result of this incident Rod has been able to help others a great deal more effectively. People facing death and all the resulting worries are comforted by the knowledge he imparts from his own experience. He is certain that this is why he was allowed to return and his ministry continues to this day. His life is as busy and full as it ever was and the memory of the day he died is as sharp as ever.

The game of tennis brings a lot of pleasure to a lot of people. Mostly I am a Wimbledon, once-a-year fan, caught up in the atmosphere of strawberries and cream and, hopefully, sunshine. Others enjoy the skill and exercise involved and regard the game as therapeutic. This was certainly the case for a friend of mine, for whom playing tennis one summer evening helped her through an emotional time in her life. Only three weeks before, Mary's much loved father had died. The shock and grief had been enormous and a game of tennis seemed a good idea to relieve the tension. She indulged in a very vigorous game and as she had hoped she felt quite tired and expected to sleep. Taking a hot soothing shower, she then fell into bed and a deep sleep. A few hours later, she woke with the most severe stomach pain. Mary's mother called the doctor, who lost no time in getting her into hospital.

Investigations at the hospital revealed that her appendix would have to be removed as a matter of urgency. She was rushed into surgery where her condition was thought to be very serious, the appendix having ruptured. Speed was of the essence, especially when they opened Mary's abdomen to find further complications. Toxaemia was feared and, following surgery, Mary was very poorly indeed. Waking to the sight and sensation of tubes everywhere was very unpleasant. She was in the intensive care unit with staff monitoring her closely. The distress to Mary's mother was hard to describe; having only recently lost her husband she faced the fact that her only child was seriously ill.

Two nights after the surgery, Mary's condition suddenly deteriorated. In retrospect she says that she was instantly aware that she was dying. There was no fear, she says, just a simple knowledge that life was coming to an end. A dark tunnel appeared in front of her; it was very long and she could see a bright light at the far end. She felt herself travel down the tunnel accompanied by low, sweet music. It was unlike any music she had heard before and really defied description, she told me. The end of the tunnel approached and she was aware of the intensity of the light. In the centre of the light was the outline of huge gates. They were arched in shape, and she found herself being propelled towards them.

There was a conscious realisation for Mary that this was in fact what it felt like to die. As if pulling herself together, she made a definite choice to resist as she decided that she did in fact want to live. Firmly and loudly she told herself, 'I am not going to die.' At that point the vision faded and she fell into a deep sleep. Like many other people who undergo these experiences, Mary kept it to herself. In her late teens, she was acutely aware that she could be laughed at or simply not believed. Many weeks later, she was home and much better, chatting to her mother about the whole episode. She decided she would tell her mother what had happened to her that night. After listening intently to her story, Mary's mother said it had been that night that the medical staff had expressed their sympathy to her. It was clear that Mary was not expected to live. The expression 'touch and go' was used several times, as her life seemed held in the balance. This confirmed the reality of the near-death experience for Mary and, far from laughing, her mother shivered at the thought of what might have been.

It was one of those days that endorsed the reputation Manchester has of Umbrella Capital of England. The rain had been falling heavily all morning, lowering the temperature and producing an enveloping grey gloom. It was obviously a day to stay indoors. John watched as his children played a game on the floor and thought that they might feel a little chilly. He decided to plug in a spare electric fire to give a boost to the heat of the room. The fire was of the type that has a light bulb to simulate glowing coals. It appeared to need a new bulb, so John brought a spare to insert at the back of the fire. Reaching to extract the spent bulb, his hand came into contact with a live wire.

His wife watched in horror as John was thrown across the room with the force of the current. The fire was still attached to his hand and from his throat came the most frightening choking noises. Hands shaking, she rang the emergency services and calmed the children, who by now realised this was not a game as they had first thought. The gravity of the situation hit John's wife as they sped to hospital in the ambulance. John was rushed into intensive care, and the staff were horrified to observe that his hand had been burnt to the bone. So far we have learned of the facts relating to this accident and the reaction of his family. What about the accident from John's perspective? The searing pain he felt was difficult to describe. This was followed by complete silence and an awareness of a huge bright light as he hovered at ceiling level. He observed the scene below him, his wife on the telephone and his children confused and tearful. Watching his body from the safety of the wonderful light he felt happy and secure. The feeling was so marvellous he did not wish to return. With great speed he suddenly found himself being thrust downwards, re-entering his body with a jolt.

John pondered on the events when he was home and well again. The fact that he had a wife and young family must have been a major factor in his return to this life, and he was happy to be with them once more. A great deal of soul-searching followed for John and his life took a more spiritual path from then on. His life had been spared and from that point it was also dramatically altered.

Near-death experiences are, one would think, exclusive to those on the brink of dying. But one perfectly healthy young lady describes undergoing a classic near-death experience. In retrospect she is convinced that this was to help her come to terms with the death of her mother. It was as if she was shown in advance where her mother would be and what she was about to experience. It certainly was a comfort when her mother passed away.

This unique account begins on what was a perfectly normal evening. Caroline went to bed and fell into a peaceful sleep almost immediately. She was woken sometime later by a vivid glowing light in her bedroom. She recalls how calm she felt, no trace of fear. From this bright glow there emerged two angels, strangely middle-aged in appearance. One always assumes angels will be young, but she says they had comfortable features, and short curly hair. Translucent skin and sparkling eyes added to their lustre. Amazing robes of white, but with a distinct blue sheen, covered them from shoulder to toe. Everything about them shimmered and glowed.

The angels told Caroline that she was to accompany them and she asked if she might say goodbye to her little girl first. She firmly believed that she was dying and happily the angels watched as she said goodbye to her sleeping daughter. Standing at the top of the stairs at this point, the angels stood on either side of Caroline, gently placing an arm across her back. How safe and secure she felt, and not at all surprised when a tunnel opened up in front of them. In the centre of a radiant light they stepped into the tunnel. Floating gently upwards Caroline was aware of the angels' robes billowing out behind them. From a gentle radiance the light grew in intensity until almost dazzling and yet it did not hurt the eyes at all. They emerged from the light into a most beautiful garden. Plants and trees were unfamiliar but exquisite, vast lawns spread in all directions and children played happily. All was bathed in a gentle glowing light. People strolled down paths to houses and it seemed a most glorious place. Caroline turned to one of her angel escorts and enquired if she was going to see Jesus. Not this time, she was informed, you now have to return. There was a rocking motion and the scene gradually faded. Caroline was now standing in her own bedroom once more. The clarity of the experience remains constant and when Caroline's mother died not too long after her visit with the angels she felt immensely comforted to have been shown by the angels where her mother had gone and where she was now surely very happy.

From the snow-capped mountains of Snowdonia to the white sand beaches of the coast, it cannot be denied that

Wales is an extremely beautiful country. Only too aware of this and fortunate enough to be living by the sea, Susan was happy. She lived in a pretty cottage with her husband, in the centre of a tiny but delightful village. Newly married and new to the area, she was at first a little lonely, missing her old life and friends in the bustle of a big city. It will take time to settle, she reasoned, but was anxious to meet more people. Several months passed before the long-awaited breakthrough came: they were invited to a party. A business contact of her husband was holding a fancy dress party and this sounded like good fun and a place for social contacts to be made. Carefully deciding on a costume and making it herself was most enjoyable and the evening would not come quickly enough. To add to the pleasure, her sister and brother-in-law decided to visit that very weekend and they were cordially invited to join the party also.

On the morning of the party Susan woke feeling a little nauseous and wondered if it might be nerves, although that would have been out of character. She took a couple of tablets and tried to forget the sensation. Her sister and brother-in-law arrived and they had a lovely day showing them the area. By early evening Susan could ignore the feelings of nausea no longer. She now had a severe stomach pain and there was nothing for it but to go and lie down. The time for the party arrived and Susan realised that she would not be able to attend. Terribly disappointed, she nevertheless insisted the others went without her and that she would be fine after a good sleep. Reluctantly they went, insisting that they would not stay late and would be home to check on her in an hour or so. The pain increased in intensity and Susan felt very ill indeed. How relieved she was to hear the sound of the car returning and her sister rushing upstairs to see how she was.

One look was enough to see how serious the situation was and an ambulance was called immediately. Susan was by now drifting in and out of consciousness and it was almost an effort to breathe. A wonderful sensation of elation suddenly engulfed Susan and the intense pain went away. It was amazing but there she was, high above the bed, watching everyone panic. She looked down on herself and noted how white her face was. Tears ran down her sister's face and the two men were in complete shock, believing Susan to be dead. Floating in a sea of love she recalls thinking, if this is dying then it is quite wonderful and I do not mind at all. Her vision then penetrated through the cottage walls and she could see the road outside. Speeding through the narrow country lanes the doctor's car and the ambulance rapidly approached. Watching with interest, she saw the doctor run inside the house and up the stairs. Swiftly taking a syringe from his bag, he filled it with a solution and injected Susan. This coincided with what Susan says she can only describe as a 'whoosh' as she catapulted back into her body.

Her next memory is of being wheeled to the operating theatre. She learned on the next morning, after recovering slightly, that sadly she had suffered an ectopic pregnancy. Her life had been saved and she was still a young woman and grateful for that. She will never forget the marvellous feelings of love and peace she encountered on that night and says how thankful she was that on the point of the most intense pain she was lifted almost to heaven.

Justine had enjoyed a very happy childhood. She was bright and strong-minded with a very positive outlook on life. Her parents and brother loved her dearly and she loved them in return, so the present and future appeared to be very sunny. Teenage years and their associated problems were made easier for Justine simply because she was able to talk to her parents about any problems that arose. Her relationship with her father was especially close and she felt secure and cherished.

Moving up the career ladder often involves long spells away from home for many career men and Justine's father was no exception. He was greatly missed but they understood when conferences and meetings kept him away from home. One day Justine's father announced that he would be attending a residential course of several weeks' duration. They all said he would be missed but were not unduly surprised. This would be beneficial for his career prospects and they assured him that they understood. The time seemed to pass very slowly and Justine found herself looking at the calendar each day and ticking off the days. It was wonderful to have him home again but they were a little confused by his demeanour. He was uncharacteristically quiet and withdrawn. Usually he would be full of stories, telling them about events and people he had met, and it all seemed rather odd. It was decided by

Justine's mother that he must be very tired from the course – he would be fine in a day or two and they must let him rest.

Days turned into weeks and there was no sign of the happy cheerful father they all knew. It was as if he had gone out of the door one person and returned completely different, everyone was terribly confused. Justine was particularly upset, she felt she could no longer talk to him, and it was as if she had lost her best friend as well as her father. With chilling suddenness he announced one day that he was leaving, this time permanently. He didn't seem to have an explanation even, just insisting that he could no longer live with them. The entire family was devastated and numb with disbelief. Justine had her seventeenth birthday but there was little joy in the day – she felt that her rock had gone and her life was crumbling away. She began to suffer from depression, incapable of understanding why the happy home she had grown up in no longer existed. It felt exactly like a bereavement and very painful.

Some time passed and one night Justine's mother was visiting a friend for the evening and her brother was away from home. Alone in the house Justine dwelled on the events of the past, and she became so distressed the thought came to her that she could no longer carry on. Suicide appeared to be the only way out of her pain. Her memory of the events that followed are just a blur and as a nightmare-like state. Her next clear memory is of staring down at her lifeless body as paramedics worked on her. She drifted in and out of this state in the ambulance all the way to the hospital. One moment she was aware of pain and movement, the next standing next to her body observing. They reached the hospital and Justine was placed on a trolley. Rushed quickly down the corridor she saw the lights passing overhead and then the most amazing event occurred. She was drawn down a long dark tunnel and saw at the far end an extremely bright light. She had an awareness that she was very close to death. The light increased in intensity and she felt no fear, only a sensation of approaching heaven. There were no figures, no voices and no music, just a gentle fading of the light and the tunnel before she found herself once more back in her body. She was in intensive care, slowly to return to health and strength.

All this seems a long time ago – she was only a teenager and now she is a happily married young lady with a family of her own. She looks back on that night with intense gratitude for having been allowed to survive. One thing remains firmly in her mind and that is the fact that death holds no fear for her any more and she faces the future with confidence.

Near-death experiences are by their very nature similar; as we have seen a tunnel and bright light usually feature. Hospitals, as we might expect, also feature strongly in the accounts. Previous stories demonstrate that this is by no means always the case. However, I should like to conclude this chapter with two brief accounts of typical experiences.

One lady is aware that as she was given strong drugs in hospital this could lead people to remark that they were certainly the origin of her experience. The other person, however, had no medication whatsoever and yet underwent a similar experience. Here are their stories.

The birth of a baby is usually the cause for celebration and although jolly hard work for the mother is usually straightforward. Occasionally things do go dangerously wrong and this was the case for Marian. Two weeks past the expected delivery date Marian was suffering dreadful pains, and in need of urgent attention she was admitted to hospital. One and a half days passed and she still felt extremely unwell. The baby and Marian were being constantly monitored and it became clear that they were approaching a critical point. An emergency caesarean operation was decided upon and Marian was wheeled down the corridor to theatre. She is, in her own mind, absolutely certain that the following events were not drug-induced. From feeling very ill and in pain, she was suddenly engulfed by a wonderful feeling of wellbeing. Down a long tunnel she went, but this was not the traditional dark tunnel. It was an amazing spiral of swirling colours and the experience was quite marvellous. Marian felt wonderful, surrounded by overwhelming feelings of peace and pure love. Arriving at the theatre, anaesthetic was administered and instantly the feelings of wellbeing went as she sank into unconsciousness. Many anxious days followed. Baby Andrew was placed in intensive care and Marian remained very poorly. Mercifully both pulled through, but Marian realises only too well how close to death she came that night and has no doubt in her mind at all that she had the most amazing near-death experience.

George waved away the sweet trolley with a groan; he could not swallow another morsel. It had been a lovely night out but he was tired and ready to sleep. Arriving home, George and his wife Christine went straight to bed, happy and content, very full, and readily fell asleep. On waking the following morning George never doubted that the pain he was feeling in his chest was indigestion. After the hearty meal he had eaten the night before it seemed obvious. However, it soon became clear that a doctor was needed, for the pain was getting much worse. The doctor felt certain that George was suffering a heart attack and he was swiftly removed to hospital.

Seriously in danger, on reaching the hospital George was immediately admitted to intensive care. He remembers nothing until waking in the intensive care room. Turning to Christine he asked the time; it was clear that he believed it to be later the same day. How amazed he was to discover that he had actually been in hospital a week! At last he was considered well enough to be transferred to a normal day ward and he declared that he was feeling much better. A couple of days passed without difficulty and Christine hoped that he would soon be home. On the third day the pain returned so violently that George could not breathe. A nurse rushed to his side and he distinctly recalls asking her to hold his hand. He obviously had a strong premonition that he was close to death. He then recalls a strange sensation of detachment and to his astonishment found himself floating near the ceiling. He was high in the corner of the room watching with interest the scene below. The crash team was working furiously to try to save his life. He could see the nurse, still holding his hand and reassuring him. In an instant George was back in his body. He tried to absorb the scene and wondered if he should tell them about his experience. How on earth can I possibly describe it, he thought. Well, he said to himself, what a story I shall have to tell Christine when she arrives today.

As a child, Rochelle had been prone to severe and prolonged bouts of tonsillitis. The recurring problem became so debilitating that it was obvious to all that the offending tonsils would have to be removed. Comfortingly, she was told that following surgery she should recover quickly and never again suffer the agonies of tonsillitis. Meanwhile long periods in bed were made less dull by her many books about the cosmos. Rochelle recalls a fascination with stars and planets from an early age. Books with pictures of the universe and maps of the stars enthralled her. Astronomy was to become a life-long passion.

When the day of her operation arrived, everyone was ill at ease, particularly Rochelle. To this day she recalls with a shiver the large mask closing over her face and chloroform being administered. There was no pre-medication to calm children in those days and so Rochelle panicked. Her parents later told her that everything did not go smoothly and that the medical staff were seriously concerned at various points during the operation.

Rochelle remembers clearly what happened next. Whilst the doctors and nurses struggled to revive her after complications, she had the most astounding near-death experience. A sensation of shooting high above the ground at tremendous speed was followed by an acute sense of loneliness, though she felt no fear. Planets and stars surrounded her as she floated looking down on the Earth below. The next thing she recalls was the nurse's voice and the realisation that she was back in her hospital bed.

As the years have passed Rochelle's interest in astronomy has grown. Many readers may feel that her near-death experience was in truth a dream induced by the chloroform and based on her love of the solar system. However, Carl Jung had a very similar experience in the days before space travel, and so did the famous children's author Enid Blyton. She wrote, 'Whilst being treated at the dentist I found myself drawn through space at a speed so great, I thought I must be going at the speed of light itself. I seemed to go through vibrating waves of light and thought I must be passing many suns and many universes.'

I have tried in this book to discover more about angels and near-death phenomena through personal experiences. Bloynan experienced out-of-body sensations and near-death experiences. Even though he was seriously ill at the time and undergoing hospital treatment, he has no doubt whatsoever that he was allowed great insight into the next world.

It was in May 1994 when his sequence of spiritual events began. Extremely ill, he had for days been drifting in and out of consciousness, when he had the sensation of 'waking up' in the next world. He was riding a horse along the edge of a field of ripe corn. Farmers were tending the crop. The colours in this scene were astonishingly bright and vibrant. Bloynan says, 'I saw substance as being made of light.' The sensation was, he said, of being in a hologram where everything was solid and yet insubstantial. He had a strong sense of the fact that everyone was doing exactly what they wished to do; there was no sense of compulsion in this world. He felt completely at home in this visionary world and it all felt more real that the familiar material world.

At this point he recognised and had conversations with his grandparents. His grandmother had died when Bloynan was only three years old and yet she was very familiar to him. They had a long and intellectual conversation, specifically about the purpose and choices of his destiny. Communication was of a telepathic nature, a condition many have reported during near-death experiences. Like so many others before him, Bloynan cannot recall the information given to him in this encounter. Bloynan's grandfather had died when he was twelve years old and he remembered him as being a rather gruff person. They got along extremely well on this occasion, having a harmonious conversation. A great sense of 'knowing' pervaded all;

everything was lucid in this place of light. His grandmother talked of the 'beings' which inhabited this beautiful place and described them as 'holy yet ineffable'. She imparted the feeling to him that despite everything all would be well with the world, saying there was a simple plan and logic to the whole of creation.

Several days after this vision of the other world, Bloynan felt himself leaving his body. He could see his physical surroundings and he describes the feeling as like taking off a heavy, thick and uncomfortable overcoat. He has the lasting impression that in fact the 'next world' is an oversimplification. There are, he says, in his experience different dimensions and levels, each with its own characteristics and laws of nature. Several more incidents and experiences happened to Bloynan during his hospitalisation. He now states that he knows that he has been allowed to visit the other world and he no longer considers it guesswork. He has seen and he certainly believes; the next world for him is simply a fact.

A severely protracted illness is difficult for anyone to endure, but when a twenty-one-year-old has to cope it is doubly difficult. Rachel had to endure the symptoms brought about by Chronic Fatigue Syndrome. This was to last for three and a half years and curtailed all the activities of a fun-loving young lady. One day proved to be the most demanding of all. Stabbing pains in her chest frightened Rachel; even the act of breathing was difficult and exacerbated the pain. At one point the pain became unbearable and it was then that she began to feel she was in fact dying. She recalls the appearance of a dark tunnel opening before her and a bluish-white light glowing at the far end. Realising with amazement that she was actually inside this tunnel, gazing towards the light, she was astonished to see a figure emerging. Instinctively Rachel knew it was her grandfather; he had been much loved, and she had missed him greatly when he died. He slowly walked from the light, looking as he had always done when alive. He was even wearing a familiar suit. It all appeared so normal and comfortable, and she was delighted to see him once more.

Standing a little way in front of Rachel, he told her that it was not in fact her time to go to heaven. Many people, he told her, would have need of her help, so she had to remain strong and never give up. This was obviously a reference to the illness she would have to face, but also an encourage-ment for her life's direction. He reached out his hand towards Rachel and she realised that this must be a gesture of farewell – she would soon have to leave this extra-ordinary place. Holding out her hand she felt her grandfather touch her finger with his own. A wonderful blue-white light radiated from him and engulfed Rachel, filling her with the most amazing sensations of peace and love. Moments later she was once more conscious of lying in her bed, but the pain and fear had subsided and she found she could breathe easily once more.

Today Rachel is much stronger and is cheerfully facing the future. She is seeking work where she can help others, offering care and support. Valuable work indeed and she knows the strength and drive to carry on came from that wonderful encounter with her grandfather and her contact with the next world. She says that she will never forget the day she and her much loved grandfather were reunited, if only for a brief moment.

✳ ✳ ✳ 9 ✳ ✳ ✳

Twin Near-death Experiences

*'We all move on the fringes of eternity and are
sometimes granted vistas through the fabric of
illusion.'*

ANSEL ADAMS

Over the past decade I must have interviewed
literally hundreds of people concerning their
spiritual experiences. Inevitably, many are very
similar in nature, especially the near-death experiences. As
we have seen these usually feature a dark tunnel, travelling
at speed and a very bright light. These basic elements have
additional features depending on the person and the
circumstances. Much rarer are the accounts of two people
sharing the same experience simultaneously. These I have
called twin near-death experiences. Not only are these
accounts fascinating but they would take some explaining
by the critics who say these experiences are all in the mind.
So many sceptics insist we are projecting the image or see
what we want to see. How two people, sometimes
separated by thousands of miles, can project the same
image is difficult to comprehend. Usually the person

experiencing the near-death experience in sympathy, as it were, has no idea that their nearest and dearest is ill.

Larry Dossey M.D., in his book *Reinventing Medicine*, talks about 'nonlocality'. Distant healing or prayer would fall into this category. He states that the minds of all humans are linked. Dream predictions, astral projection and near-death twinning give credence to this theory. Consciousness exists outside the body; time and distance are not relevant. Food for thought as we contemplate the following remarkable stories.

Occasionally a story reaches me that is so different in every aspect, I can only marvel at it. One such story is Mark's. It is the first time I have ever encountered communication by two people simultaneously out of their bodies. This is a heart-warming and unique story and the events changed Mark's life for ever. Talking to Mark, one is aware of just how well balanced and normal he is. An everyday person to whom extraordinary events happened. He was only seven years old at the time, and now he is in his mid-thirties the emotions are still very close to the surface and the memory as clear as ever.

As the youngest child in a large family, he recalls growing up amid fun and laughter. They were very happy years and he was especially close to his two sisters, who were only a little older than he. A favourite pastime, as with many children, was to arrange impromptu concerts. They would sing and dance in turn and award each other points. It being the seventies, space travel was very much in the news. Mark was fascinated. He had been given a space outfit complete with helmet and many of his song and dance routines were performed in this costume. They had a 'stage' in one of the bedrooms which was in fact a large chest of drawers. Each child would climb on top of the chest in turn and perform their act.

One day the children decided to hold a concert and when it was Mark's turn he scrambled on top of the furniture eager to perform his act. Placing his space helmet at his feet, he started to dance with enthusiasm. Kicking his foot to the beat of the music, he suddenly caught the helmet and this in turn sent him hurtling forwards. Losing his balance completely he found himself colliding with the very hard surface of the wooden bed, instantly knocking himself out. His distraught family rushed him to hospital where he underwent many tests. As he regained consciousness the doctors appeared to be very concerned. His blood pressure was extremely high and his kidneys were not functioning properly. On the X-ray, they could only see one kidney and that appeared far from healthy. It seemed that the accident had brought him to the hospital just in time for medical treatment that was urgently required.

Attaching Mark to a dialysis machine the physicians at St Mary's Hospital in Portsmouth decided that he must be included on the list for a kidney transplant. Mark was very ill indeed at this point and remained so for several days before a gradual improvement took place. All the results of the tests were now available and to everyone's amazement the figures were completely reversed. Not only was his blood pressure normal, but his kidney function had vastly improved and most amazing of all there appeared to be another kidney visible on the X-ray. To say the doctors were confused by this bizarre situation would be an understatement and they immediately ordered the whole set of tests to be repeated. Every possible explanation was considered. Was the equipment faulty? It did not seem likely; it was the newest available and had certainly never failed before. Human error was eliminated when the second set of tests was studied. It was all most bewildering.

It was at this point that, to everyone's dismay, Mark fell into a coma. Totally unexpected, it confused the medical staff even more, and threw Mark's worried parents onto an emotional roller coaster. Sitting by his bed in great distress they found it difficult to comprehend what was happening. At precisely this time Mark's experiences began. Initially he recalls a typical out-of-body experience. He was looking down on his comatose form on the bed, noting the tears running down his father's face and his mother holding his hand. Glancing round he noticed that his bed was one of two in a small room. Leading from this room was a door opening into a children's playroom. The occupant of the bed opposite to Mark was another young boy. He had obviously suffered terrible head injuries and was in considerable pain. His crying was heart-breaking and Mark felt great concern for this little boy. To Mark's surprise the door to the playroom slowly opened of its own accord. Time did not seem to be relevant but Mark noted that it must be night because the playroom was in darkness.

Entering the room he became fascinated by the branches of a large tree, tapping against the window in the wind. The tree was silhouetted against the night sky and the only light came from the gentle glow of a street lamp. Mesmerised, Mark watched as a figure emerged from the dark centre of the tree. The figure then literally passed through the window into the room. Normally one would expect a small boy to be terrified by this event, but in fact the reverse happened. An overwhelming feeling of love and happiness surged through him. The atmosphere in the room was of sheer peace and even at the tender age of seven Mark found himself thinking that this must be what heaven feels like. The shape he now recalls was definitely female but was not accompanied by the usual bright light. The being then spoke and Mark recalls it was as if ripples were passing through him. He was engulfed by the vibrations of this voice that seemed to affect every cell in his body. How wonderful he felt and especially so when the being said to him that he was not to worry about dying. He must tell his distressed parents that he would be well again and certainly was not going to die. For an instant there was a feeling of being granted knowledge beyond his years, sensations of knowing swept over him as he listened to this wonderful being.

Turning his head Mark became conscious of another figure in the room. This third figure was in fact the little boy from the bed opposite Mark's. Looking back into the little room they could see both their forms lying on the beds. Both were out of their bodies, much to their amazement. How delighted Mark was to see the little boy smiling happily and completely free from pain. They found communicating very easy and even indulged in game … Slowly the shadow figure retreated towards the window once more. Quickly Mark asked, 'Who are you?' and was stunned by the answer 'God'. The face became clear and Mark thought now that this was Jesus. The young boy was perplexed; he had never entertained religious thoughts. Nor had he ever received religious instruction. How did he know or recognise the face as that of Jesus? He could only gaze awe-struck as the figure melted once more into the dark swaying branches of the tree outside.

Opening his eyes at this point he realised that he was once more in his body. It was now daylight and he saw his mother arrive at the door of the little ward. How delighted she was to see her son awake and looking so much better. Now fully awake and aware of some pain, Mark went over the events of the night in his head. You may consider, as indeed Mark did, that this was a dream. He tried to make sense of it all, but could not shake off the conviction that this was indeed real, he was absolutely sure it had happened. He glanced across the room to the bed opposite. The little boy was not there. 'Has my friend gone home?' he asked his mother. 'No, dear,' she answered softly. 'Sadly the little boy died during the night.'

This fact convinced Mark that the events of the night were real. He knew for certain then that it had not been a dream but that he really had been out of his body. Over the years many questions about that night have entered his head. This is the one memory from his childhood that remains crystal-clear. This is the case with so many people who have spiritual experiences in childhood. The normal everyday memories are now hazy but not only is the amazing sight he saw clear in his mind, but also the sensations and emotions he felt. It is no exaggeration to say that Mark's life has been deeply affected by this event. He has an unshakeable belief in the afterlife and a strong sense of protection at all times. He continues to be remarkably healthy, although still on medication for his kidney complaint. Recently his routine check and tests revealed that he continues to improve. The normal pattern of someone who has been suffering a kidney complaint from childhood would be steady deterioration. Once more the tests were repeated to be absolutely sure of the results. Why he is not permanently using a dialysis machine and on the list for a transplant is a mystery the medical team cannot understand. No longer baffled by events, Mark is simply grateful to have been so blessed.

It had been a gloriously hot summer, Pamela loved the heat but she loved the evenings especially; they were, she says, magic. On this particular evening Pamela carried a tray into the garden with a pot of tea and a large chocolate cake which they were going to eat for dessert. Greg, her husband, sat under the trees reading the evening news-paper, their dog Fred at his feet. Soon Fred would pester for an evening walk but at the present moment he snored happily in the late sunshine. It was wonderful to step out into the garden, Pamela thought, after a lifetime of flat-dwelling. Greg had been a journalist on a large city newspaper and they had always lived in the heart of London. Windowboxes were the nearest thing to a garden they had ever possessed. Moving to the countryside when they reached retirement had been a blessing and they thoroughly enjoyed it. The only drawback was the fact that they were now a long way from Pamela's elderly parents who still lived in a London suburb. They managed a monthly visit to check on them and so far everything seemed to be going well.

The long summer evening was finally coming to a close and twilight fell. Greg took the dog for a walk and Pamela, reluctant to go indoors, sat soaking up the smell of night-scented stock. A feeling of anxiety suddenly overcame her and to her amazement there appeared in front of her a dark tunnel. Bombarded by small spheres of light, she had the sensation of moving at speed through this tunnel before her. Emerging from the tunnel, in a blaze of light she saw her father; he was sitting with a red cloak around his shoulders. He held out his arms towards her and she bent to hug him. At this moment the chair was pulled backwards and he faded from view. The feeling of speed returned, and in an instant she was sitting once more beneath the tree in her own garden. It was the oddest thing that had ever happened to her, she thought, and although she considered the possibility of a dream or hallucination she knew in her heart it was neither of these.

Arriving home, her husband remarked how light it still was for 9.30 pm. Seeing his wife a little distressed he asked what the matter was. He listened carefully but did not dismiss the story as a dream or hallucination. 'It sounds like a classic near-death experience,' he said. Concerned, Pamela rushed to phone her parents but was surprised to find the answerphone switched on. Where could they be at this time of night, she thought. Only a moment later Pamela's mother rang. She explained that she was at the hospital, where they had been taken by ambulance because Pamela's father had suffered a heart attack. 'How is he?' they asked fearfully. 'I am assured he will be fine,' Pamela's mother replied. 'It was frightful at the time,' she added, 'to see him wheeled out of the house swathed in a huge red blanket.' Pamela gasped. 'What time was this?' she asked. 'Around 9.30 pm,' her mother replied. Pamela then had no doubt in her mind that she had actually experienced the near-death phenomenon with her father.

It is true to say that many of us do not realise just how much we love someone, especially, it seems, our parents, until we lose them. The following story is a prime example of this fact.

No doubt about it, Rosemary loved her father, but the fact remained that he was a difficult person to get close to. He was a clever, articulate man, well respected by all who knew him. Extremely private by nature, he found it difficult to unbend. However, he positively adored children and found communication with them both simple and a joy. As Rosemary grew older, the closeness she yearned for largely eluded her. Many times she resorted to prayer for help in becoming closer to her father, hoping to make the link between them stronger.

In time Rosemary became a mother, and she saw once

again how easily her father responded to little ones. The grandchildren grew and Rosemary watched her father ageing. No one was prepared for the shock when one day he suffered a severe stroke. It was the start of many long days spent in three different hospitals without any sign of significant improvement in her father's health. Eventually he was admitted to the local hospital and this meant an easier journey and more frequent visits by Rosemary and her mother.

One day, having spent hours by his bedside, they returned home only to receive a phone call saying that Rosemary's father had died. Rosemary later calculated that an extraordinary event had occurred at precisely the moment of her father's death. Sitting in warm sunshine, taking tea in a friend's garden, Rosemary's daughter and her husband saw a huge bright light in front of them. No figure appeared, but they knew instantly that this was Grandfather saying goodbye. The most amazing fact is that although he had died in Devon, England, Rosemary's daughter and husband were in a garden in Seattle on the Northwest Coast of the USA.

Some time later, during an operation, Rosemary's daughter saw her grandfather standing by the bed. This time he was plainly visible and she knew that he was taking care of her and her wellbeing. Rosemary has had a number of similar experiences and unusual feelings that indicate her father's presence. She has even received advice from him in dreams, making him feel very close to her. It is as if death freed him from the constraints of his earthly personality and they are now as close as Rosemary always wished to be.

*'A cluster of white stars, silvered against the
background of the blue velvet sky, force their way into
my eyes and into my heart.'*

MARC CHAGALL

To gaze up into a clear night sky, far away from city light,
and see the stars can be a breathtaking experience. Man has
always looked to the stars for inspiration and guidance. The
ancients built the pyramids by star maps. The Bible tells the
story of Jesus' birth with the stars featuring prominently.
The star of David is a precious symbol to people of the
Jewish faith all over the world.

For one young lady, stars have been a big influence
throughout her life. Her parents had always been keen
astronomers and had christened their first daughter Stella.
Surrounded by charts and picture books about stars, Stella
and her sister grew up with considerable knowledge of the
universe. Visits to Jodrell Bank in the Cheshire countryside
inspired them even further to love stars and planets. The
girls had a cousin of similar age named Helen and she would
often join them on these outings. The girls grew and when
Stella left home to attend university her cousin Helen
announced that she would be taking a gap year in Australia.
So many young people today travel for a year before
university and Australia appears to be a favourite
destination. Assured by Stella that she would be dreadfully
missed Helen set off with promises of many cards, letters
and e-mails whenever possible.

Stella was not disappointed; true to her word Helen
stayed closely in touch. A trip to the outback, camping

under the stars, had proved to be the highlight of the trip so far, she told Stella. Her description of the southern sky and the stars made Stella long to be with her and she vowed that one day she would travel to Australia. Winter arrived in England and Stella tried to picture Helen celebrating Christmas in the heat of a Sydney summer. The celebrations for Stella were subdued by a nasty cold that made her feel miserable. Despite the festivities she decided on an early night. Clutching a hot-water bottle, Stella snuggled down in her bed. However, sleep would not come and Stella tossed and turned for hours. As the night wore on Stella was aware of a feeling of unease; it was not simply that she felt unwell, it was real anxiety. Puzzled, she sat up in bed; she was unaware of anything worrying her. Opening her bedroom curtains she looked up at a very clear starry night. Usually this was guaranteed to lift her spirits.

Much to her amazement she suddenly had the sensation of moving at great speed towards the night sky. Ahead of her was an incredibly bright light and hundreds of stars, unlike any she had ever seen from Earth. A voice whispered into her ear that she must not be anxious or afraid, all would be well. She found herself back in her bedroom, sitting up in bed as before. The room was just as it always was and through the opened curtains the sky with its stars appeared perfectly normal. Could I possibly have imagined all that, she thought, and yet it felt very real. All feelings of unease and anxiety had gone by now and she slipped into a deep sleep.

Twenty-four hours later, Stella's family received a

phone call from Helen's parents. They were dreadfully upset to have heard from a hospital in Sydney that Helen had been admitted to hospital suffering from meningitis. She had arrived at the hospital dangerously ill and the feeling was they had caught her just in time to save her life. She was as yet extremely poorly but the opinion was that she would pull through. Stella did some calculations based on the times her aunt and uncle had given them. It would have been exactly the time of her amazing experience that Helen was being admitted to hospital. It accounts for the feeling of anxiety and unease, she thought. Eventually, Helen was much improved and Stella was able to talk to her on the telephone. During their conversation Stella told her of the incident that night and how she had been so anxious. Helen told Stella that whilst she had been so very ill she had actually had a classic near-death experience. A true example of two people, very close by nature and yet geographically far apart, undergoing twin experiences.

✳✳✳ 10 ✳✳✳

Messages in Dreams

*'Once a dream did weave a shade o'er my
angel-guarded bed.'*

WILLIAM BLAKE

I t has been estimated that by the time we are middle-
aged we shall have spent five years dreaming. We
actually sleep for a third of our lifetime, and we
therefore spend a great deal of time in this other world of
dreams. Everyone is aware of the giants of dream
interpretation, Sigmund Freud and Carl Gustav Jung.
Their interpretations did differ somewhat but interestingly
Jung believed dreams to contain a strong spiritual element.
Keeping a dream diary has proved useful for many people.
A diary may reveal insights into the subconscious. Patterns
emerge over a period of time that may lead us down paths
unconsidered in our waking state. Prophetic dreams are
fascinating and it is not uncommon for a person to dream
of an event before it actually happens. Messages are given
in dreams but so often we fail to read them because they are
in symbolic form. There are many books available to help
one interpret dreams but often the dream is lucid and

obvious. I was once acquainted with a young lady who told me she had fallen out with her family at one point. Vowing never to speak to them again she moved apartments and got on with her life for some six months without contact. One night she had a vivid dream; an angel told her that she must go home, her sister needed her. The next day she promptly went home to discover that her sister was in fact dying of cancer and longed to see her – an amazingly lucid message. Anita also had a dream so clear that she could not fail to read the significance of it and is grateful to this day. Here is her story.

All over the United Kingdom, households were preparing for Christmas. Some people were to celebrate in their own homes while others would travel to family and friends for the holiday. As usual there would be a great criss-crossing of the country as a large proportion of the population would be on the move. Anita and her family would be travelling to Lancashire from their Yorkshire home for the big day. They were happy and excited at the thought of seeing the family and spending this special time with them. On Christmas Eve Anita's husband left the house early to complete his outstanding jobs at work so that they would be able to leave early for the journey to Lancashire. He tiptoed from the house leaving his wife and daughter fast asleep.

Meanwhile Anita had a dream unfolding in her head that would save all their lives. The vivid dream was of the family driving to the home of her parents. As the dream progressed they spotted a large, navy blue, soft-top car. It was travelling in the right-hand lane. The car had a large very distinctive badge signifying its make but Anita could not recognise it. Suddenly this car cut in front of them, directly in their path, completely without warning and the inevitable collision followed. Thrown forwards with force Anita felt the safety belt tighten on her chest with a jolt. Waking at this point she realised that she has been physically thrown forwards in bed, with the sensation of the tightening seatbelt on her chest. Heart pounding, she went over the details of the dream; its clarity was amazing and she thought it quite extraordinary.

The day passed in busy preparation. When Anita's husband arrived home they all three loaded the car with parcels and provisions for the journey. They set off singing 'Jingle Bells' and giggling like schoolchildren. They were happy and excited and thoroughly looking forward to their Christmas-time. After roughly half an hour of driving, Anita noticed with a shiver a car directly in front of them. It was large, navy blue and had a soft top. The large distinctive badge on the car was now recognisable as a Rover. The dream replayed in her head and she felt compelled to relate it to her husband. 'I feel quite spooked,' she said. 'This car is identical to the one in my dream.' Wisely her husband decided to err on the side of caution. He was driving a powerful car on an area of road with a sixty-mile-an-hour speed limit and he was doing exactly that speed. Slowing down he kept plenty of distance between himself and the car in front.

Extra vigilant, he was aware of every movement. Three miles down the road they approached a roundabout and noted that the driver of the blue car seemed a little confused and hesitant. He must have been unsure of the way for he turned right, accelerating as he did so then suddenly changed his mind and his lane, veering back directly in front of the family. Virtually prepared for this, Anita's husband avoided what could have been a dreadful accident. There is no doubt in Anita's mind that the dream was a clear warning; she also believes it was sent by the angels. Every day she thanks them for their deliverance.

Irena's dream was very different from Anita's, not one of warning but one of great insight. I first met Irena when she came to England from Russia to attend a course. A powerful personality and full of energy and zest for life, she was interested in all things spiritual. We chatted one day about the afterlife, in which she said she had an unshakeable belief. This belief had been reinforced by a remarkable dream. She had had a dearly loved aunt with whom she had shared a close relationship. As a child she felt she could trust her implicitly, and she would confide in her. As an adult Irena and her aunt lived some distance apart and she was not able to see her as often as she wished. But rarely a week went by without a telephone conversation and Irena thought of her as her rock.

One evening Irena was trying to catch up with a mountain of paperwork and the hour became very late. She found it difficult to concentrate on that particular night and for some reason felt very restless. Finally she gave up on the task and went to bed, eventually drifting off to sleep in the early hours of the morning. The dream she had that night was the most unusual she had ever experienced. She found herself alone in a large, beautiful house. She sensed a deeply spiritual atmosphere and all around was golden light. She saw in the corner of the room a heavy wooden door and made her way towards it. It required a great deal of strength to open but she felt compelled to do so. The scene that met her eyes on opening the door was astonishing. Outside the door was a long silver staircase, filled with people slowly climbing to the top. The very top of the stairs was obscured by an extremely bright light and as the people reached the top stair they were totally engulfed by this light. Looking downwards she saw her aunt start to climb towards her up the stairs. Irena stared transfixed as she climbed ever nearer. How happy she looked, smiling broadly at Irena. As she approached, Irena rushed forward to hug her aunt tightly. The aunt responded, hugging her also before gently pushing her away and continuing the climb. Irena grabbed her aunt's hand. 'Let me come with you,' she said. Firmly but kindly the aunt answered, 'No, my dear, it is not yet your time.' Gently removing her hand from Irena's she turned and continued her journey upwards. Watching her, Irena noticed that she climbed without a backward glance until she entered the light.

On waking, Irena found herself in tears but told herself firmly that it had only been a dream. Wrapping her warm dressing gown around her she went into the kitchen to make her morning cup of tea. The phone rang. It was Irena's mother. Surprised to receive a call so early in the morning she asked anxiously if she was well. 'I am fine, dear,' came the answer. 'I am ringing to tell you that your aunt died during the night.'

> *'Pass in, pass in,' the angels say,*
> *'Into the upper doors,*
> *Nor count compartments of the floors,*
> *But mount to paradise,*
> *By the stairway of surprise.'*
>
> RALPH WALDO EMERSON

We have another example of a powerful and clear dream from Charles. A Nigerian living in London with his family, he had amazing dreams surrounding the birth of his children. In July 1995, Charles was eagerly awaiting the birth of his first baby. Not knowing the sex of the baby he and his wife spent hours discussing both boys' and girls' names. The Nigerian tradition dictates that the grandparents choose the baby's name and so the whole family eagerly awaited the birth. Two weeks before the baby was due Charles was asleep one night when he began to dream. A tall man approached Charles. He wore a long white gown and carried a baby in his arms. He spoke to Charles, telling him that he was holding his little daughter and her name was Dumebi. The features of the little girl were very distinct and Charles woke with this lovely picture in his mind.

The baby duly arrived and was indeed a little girl. When Charles saw her he recognised at once the baby from his dream. The following day he went to visit his mother and was feeling a little anxious. She was after all entitled to choose a name for the little girl and yet the dream seemed to hold great significance. Imagine his surprise when his mother announced that his daughter's name would be Dumebi. It was clearly angel-inspired and he was extremely happy.

Two years later, Charles and his wife were again waiting for the birth of a baby. Astonishingly, the same angel appeared to Charles in a dream. This time he told him the baby would be a boy. There would, he said, be problems and complications but eventually all would be well and he was not to worry. The labour was indeed long and Charles told his wife what the angel had said – all would be well. Eventually Charles was told by the doctors that they would have to perform an emergency caesarean operation and would he please sign the consent form. He watched anxiously as his wife was rushed to theatre. A close friend and one of his relatives were with him to lend support. Roman Catholics, they took out their rosary beads and began to pray, asking for God's help. The doors of the waiting room opened and the doctor emerged. 'Congratulations,' he said. 'You have a little boy.' Relief flooded through Charles but he was still anxious about his wife. On rushing to her side he was delighted to find her safe and well and was informed that the operation had gone smoothly. Charles and his family feel blessed and grateful for these amazing events.

Life for the old man had become a struggle. A long and happy marriage had ended with the death of his wife and he could scarcely cope. He had no idea how he could face the future without his life-long partner. There were few people he felt he could confide in and he was at a loss as to where to turn. Years ago he had attended a church and he found himself wondering if he might find a little comfort there.

One night he had the most beautiful dream in which a little girl spoke to him. She told him that he must go back to his church and she smiled with encouragement. She wore a dazzling white dress and held a bunch of large white flowers. Not having too much knowledge in this area he had no idea what the flowers might be, simply that they were extremely beautiful, like the little girl. Twice more in the space of a week he had the same dream, each time the child insisting he attend the church. Fascinated, the old man vowed that he would make the journey to his old place of worship the very next Sunday.

Some miles away Irene was gathering her thoughts about the following Sunday service and pondering on the subject of her address. The church she had been invited to speak at was unfamiliar to her and she thought carefully about the content of her address. She would have to drive some distance, so to ensure that she would be on time she left home rather early. On her arrival only the caretaker was to be seen and he let her into the little church with a smile. I can have a few moments of quiet, Irene thought, and go over the service one more time. The time for the service arrived but no congregation and as the minutes ticked by Irene began to feel a little irritated. All her careful preparation, as well as driving miles from her home, and no one was going to come! It was an uncomfortable, sinking feeling and she was just about to leave when slowly the large front door opened. In walked the old man, who was as surprised and confused as Irene to see the place empty. It had taken quite a bit of courage to come at all, he told Irene. Soon he found himself telling Irene his problems and it became clear to her that he was desperate for a friend to listen. Could it be that this was arranged from above, she thought. After all, I could not have listened to this under normal circumstances.

Kind and sensitive, Irene listened to the old man. A calm descended on the man's face as the burden seemed to lift from him. He quite truthfully said that often it is easier to talk to a complete stranger under such circumstances. Eventually the old man stood up, preparing to leave. He thanked her profusely for her care and concern, assuring her that he felt so much better. It is as if this was meant to be, he said. He then told her about the recurring dream with the little girl and the flowers. Irene smiled; she felt a presence she had experienced many times before. His description of the child and the flowers left her in no doubt. She told the old man that her beloved granddaughter had died some years earlier and since then she had felt her presence on many occasions. There was always the feeling that she was near. 'She was the angel helping you this week,' said Irene, 'and do you know why I am so sure? Her name is Lily.' Interestingly enough, in the language of flowers the lily means life after death!

Grace had always longed to live by the sea, but it appeared to be her lot that she should sojourn in land-locked Sheffield. The whole project seemed to be impractical, and the kind of property she craved, out of her financial league. Following the death of her parents, there was a fleeting moment when she thought it might be possible. The legacy was not enormous but would make life a little more comfortable. Her needs were quite frugal; living alone, as she had for most of her adult life, she did not have an extravagant lifestyle. Her career had been very fulfilling and she had been fortunate to travel quite a bit, but now retirement drew near and she felt it would be wonderful to realise her dream. A talented painter and potter, visions of a workroom with a view of the ocean tantalised her thoughts.

For many months following her retirement Grace searched for the cottage of her dreams. Juggling with finances for hours on end, she decided that her pension and the legacy from her parents would be just enough to make the whole project possible. Time ticked away and although she searched continuously, a feasible dwelling did not appear. Her hopes were raised one day when the exact cottage she had visualised for so long came on the market. It was small but compact and had the most wonderful sea views. A long attic room would be perfect for her crafts and in short she fell in love with it. Sadly it was just beyond her range and although she kept in touch with the owners and the estate agent, hoping for a miracle, it simply did not happen.

Overcome with disappointment, Grace decided to give

up. How foolish, she thought, to think that I might achieve such an idyllic dream. All notions of moving were pushed out of her mind and she settled to the idea that she would stay land-locked permanently. A year passed and although she was quite happy in her retired life, from time to time the old yearnings crossed her mind. One night she had the most amazing dream, quite the most lucid she could ever remember. She stood outside the little seaside cottage she had once set her heart on. The door opened wide and a jolly red-haired lady welcomed her inside with a huge smile on her face. Entering the room she noticed how unusual the windows were, round like portholes, and one actually had a stained-glass replica of a sailing ship inserted into it. How beautiful, she thought, and felt confused as to why she had not noticed the wonderful windows in the estate agent's brochure.

Waking the following morning, she found herself in tears. I had forgotten how strong my feelings had been about that little cottage, she thought. A little later in the morning, Grace sat down with a cup of coffee, lost in thought. She suddenly jumped as the phone rang, and was even more surprised to hear the voice of the estate agent. 'The little cottage you were interested in is back on the market,' he said. Grace held her breath as he explained that shortly after she had given up the idea of purchase the people had taken the cottage off the market, deciding not to move after all. Circumstances had recently changed dramatically, and due to a family crisis they would need to move as quickly as possible. The price was now probably within her range he said, and asked if she would like to have another look.

Trembling with excitement, Grace walked up the path to the little cottage. Astonishingly, the door was opened by a lady with a cascade of red hair. Smiling warmly at Grace she led the way into the little room. There to Grace's surprise was a round window with a beautiful stained-glass sailing ship in its centre. She had no need to think twice about buying the house, the signs had been so obvious in her dream. She had such a feeling of coming home. There can be no truer expression, she thought, than 'Follow your dream'.

* * ✴ 11 ✴ * *

Look for a Sign

'It is to those who perceive through symbols, the poets,
the artists, and seekers for meaning, that the angel
makes himself known.'

THEODORA WARD

We are constantly surrounded by signs. Their messages, particularly from the source of nature, can be pertinent and helpful. Sadly we appear to have lost the ability to read them. Ancient peoples lived their lives by nature's signs. Denise Lynn in her wonderful book *Signposts* says, 'The universe is whispering to you.' Science and technology dominated the twentieth century and our awareness of spiritual signs became lost in this dazzling new world. If we consider the damage we are inflicting on the planet, it would appear to be very timely that we are listening to nature once more. Instinctively we are looking for inspiration in the natural world. The current love of gardening, promoted by so many television programmes, is indicative of a search for peace and spirituality through sheer beauty. It is a search for calm amongst the frenetic pace of life.

The most important element in receiving help and comfort from a sign is that of timing. When seeing a sign, the actual moment is the all-important factor. Paul McCartney recently spoke of feeling the presence of his deceased wife Linda amongst the birds and animals that visited his garden. He describes the hoot of an owl as being most significant at special times. He has very movingly written poetry about such events.

Symbols, like angels, can appear in our lives so subtly that we have to concentrate in order to read the signs. Often when we focus on them they will become more obvious and happen more frequently.

One young lady told me that when working abroad she became very homesick. She realised one day that whenever she felt particularly low a letter or card from home would arrive. If she was thinking about a particular friend or family member there would be a phone call from that person. It occurred to her that maybe an angel was helping her and so she meditated and the name Rose came into her head. Could this be the name or the symbol of her angel? She walked upstairs in the house where she was staying and her host's two young daughters, both in separate rooms, came to greet her. They had been painting, and each had a picture especially for her. Each child had painted a rose! On the same day a younger child was playing with a box full of coloured stickers. 'I want you to have one,' the child said, and from a selection of at least a hundred handed her the sticker of a rose. Reflecting on all this she went for an evening walk, and her gaze was drawn to the top window of a house she had passed many times. Gleaming ruby red in the late sunshine was a beautiful stained-glass rose. Wonderful confirmation for the young lady that she was actually tuning in to her angel.

I have heard many stories about symbolism and death, but I feel that Evangeline's tale is probably unique. Evangeline had a great deal to look forward to: soon it would be her seventeenth birthday, Christmas was on the way, and a new baby was expected in the family at around the same time. The whole family was eagerly awaiting this event.

Excitement was mounting as 21 December arrived. Intending to go out on a shopping trip, Evangeline ran downstairs happily, clutching her bag. On reaching the door, she realised that she had forgotten something, and so raced back up the stairs. At the top, she stopped still in her tracks, astonished at the sight that met her.

In the bedroom that Evangeline shared with her sisters, there was a beautiful picture on the wall. This depicted Jesus with his arms outstretched, welcoming the little children. When the light on the landing was switched off, a reflection of the picture could be seen on the wall opposite. But, in the place of Jesus, this familiar picture now showed a bright angel, who stood with one finger pointing upwards as if to heaven. There must be a rational explanation, Evangeline reasoned. Switching off the landing light, she effectively eliminated a possible trick in the reflection as a cause. Taking a duster, she then wiped the picture vigorously, but the image remained. With a sudden instinctive knowledge, Evangeline felt sure that this was a warning, that somebody was going to die. Although it was an immense burden to her, she felt that she ought to keep the warning a secret and not alarm the rest of her family, especially not her mother who was in the final stages of pregnancy.

The angel remained in the picture until 24 December when, to Evangeline's amazement, the vision changed. In place of the angel, there was now a stark, black cross. Fear gripped the young girl every time that a family member left the house: she was convinced that she would never see them again. Bravely, she kept her mounting worries to herself.

Christmas passed and 27 December arrived, bringing with it Evangeline's birthday. This was when her mother was taken to hospital to deliver the new baby. The other children waited eagerly at home for news. Eventually their father arrived back but one look at his face told them that all was not well. He told them sadly that a beautiful little girl had been born but that she had died shortly afterwards. Thankfully, their mother was physically well and would be home with them all shortly.

Slowly trying to absorb this news, Evangeline climbed the stairs to her room. As she had suspected, the picture was now completely back to normal, Jesus once more holding out his arms to receive little ones. He has, she thought, received my baby sister. She wondered if, as the eldest child in the family, she had been forewarned about the death so as to enable her to be strong and help her mother. One amazing fact, however, is that this very brave young lady kept her extraordinary story to herself for many years.

The symbol in our next story is perhaps the least likely object to be thought spiritual, namely an electric kettle, but angels, like God, work in mysterious ways. Here is the story of a young mother struggling to come to terms with bereavement.

Walking the children to school used to be such fun for Donna. They lived in a pleasant leafy road, and at each corner the little group grew in number. Other children and their mothers joined the group until at last, arriving at the school, they would be a large, chattering, laughing crowd. This was the original 'walking bus' before it had been thought of! Since the sudden death of Donna's husband, however, walking to school had become a trial. People are often uncertain of how to cope in such situations and Donna found herself the recipient of sympathetic glances, awkward silences or even being avoided altogether. Although Donna understood the other mothers' dilemma it was painful for her. It had been a shock to the whole community; everyone found it hard to believe that a strong thirty-year-old man should die of a heart attack.

Several months passed and Donna still felt lonely and vulnerable; trying to be strong for the children was a strain. The person who appeared to understand her most of all was her kindly, elderly, next-door neighbour. Frequently Donna would pop into her house for a heart-to-heart talk and often would feel much better afterwards. One particular morning, after dropping the children off at school, Donna went straight to her neighbour's house. The need for a chat was overwhelming and her kind neighbour, Betty, greeted her warmly. Following Betty into the kitchen, Donna sank into the comfortable chair and started to cry. She told Betty that not only was she feeling lonely but also a little guilty. The thought had crossed her mind that perhaps one day she might meet another man and re-marry. This felt like a betrayal and it distressed her greatly. 'How I wish I could talk it through with my husband,' she said. 'When we had a problem he would say, "Put the kettle on and we'll have a cup of tea and a chat."' Laughing through her tears, Donna said, 'He thought a cup of tea would resolve anything.'

At this point, the kettle, situated at least six feet away from the two women, switched on! 'I think there is your answer,' Betty said. 'I do not think he would wish you to be alone. We shall follow his advice and make a cup of tea and talk about it.'

Birds have been considered as spiritual messengers since ancient times. The symbolism of flight and freedom is familiar to us all. Doves have always been a symbol of peace and from ancient times birds of all types have featured in paintings and literature. Even our common everyday saying 'a little bird told me' comes from the Bible. It appears that robins especially are meaningful. They arrive with such poignant timing that the symbolism is patently obvious. I receive many stories featuring robins from readers of my books. I have chosen a small sample to share with you.

It is a widely held belief that many people actually 'choose' when to die. We are all familiar with stories of people who are terminally ill surviving against all odds to attend an important event. It may be the wedding of a much loved child, the birth of a baby and so on. Sheer will power ensures that they will be present. Frequently the person will rally and enjoy the occasion immensely only to pass gently away soon after.

Christine felt that her mother, Elsie, made this choice. In November 2000 Elsie suffered a stroke. This was debilitating and a heartbreaking event for the whole family. As Elsie needed help at hand virtually round the clock, it became evident that a nursing home would be the only option. Reluctantly Elsie moved. It distressed everyone involved but the family had to accept that they could not provide the degree of care she needed. As a nurse Elsie was fully aware of her physical capabilities and what the future might hold. Relinquishing her independence was terribly sad and she was in fact very unhappy.

Shortly before Christmas, when Elsie had regained some of her former strength, she announced that she was going on holiday. She allayed everyone's fears by assuring them that she was not intending to go far: the nearby coast had a wonderful hotel where her every need would be catered for. Organised festivities in the evening would cheer her considerably, she felt. She arrived at the hotel cheerfully determined to enjoy every minute. What a wonderful week Elsie had, indulging herself in all the forbidden foods, drinking prohibited drinks and joining in all the fun. Christine was astonished to learn that her mother had actually danced for the first time in years and found it a wonderful tonic. Never in bed before midnight, it was as if Elsie had been miraculously transported back to her youth.

In early January, Elsie suffered a second, more severe stroke. She was dreadfully ill and it was unlikely she would recover a second time. At 7 am on the morning following the stroke, the family was summoned to the hospital. The staff met them with the news that Elsie was fading and they had decided her family should be with her. Grateful, Christine and her brothers sat in the little hospital room with their mother. Time passed and the family realised that they were very thirsty and a little hungry, having rushed from their homes without even a drink. Elsie appeared to be stable so they decided to pop out for ten minutes or so to find a cup of tea. When they returned to the little room they were told by a nurse, 'Your mother's gone.'

The events of the next few minutes will stay with Christine throughout her life. Bending low to say goodbye to her mother, she was astonished to see Elsie struggle to open her eyes and turn her head towards her daughter. Sighing heavily she then passed away. It was as if she had forced herself to come back to see the family one last time. There then followed an atmosphere of peace in that little room which Christine finds almost impossible to describe. 'Amazing, overwhelming peace,' she told me, and I was reminded of the biblical saying 'peace which passeth all understanding'. Science-based, Christine is a radiographer, and she is very much a practical, down-to-earth lady. Nevertheless she is aware that this experience was not of this world. On reflection it was obvious to Christine that her mother had chosen to have a short time enjoying herself to the full rather than spend the rest of her days in a nursing home. Elsie was a spirited and very brave lady.

That night, unsurprisingly, sleep would not come. Christine lay awake wondering why she had even gone to bed at all. In the early hours she gave in and went downstairs. Making a cup of tea she then took it into the conservatory to sit and look out on the garden. To her surprise it was snowing heavily. The garden looked so beautiful covered in a thick blanket of snow. Against the backdrop of a dramatically black sky, huge flakes drifted down. The scene was magical and Christine stared, transfixed by the beauty of it all. A sudden movement caught her attention; turning her head she was scarcely able to believe her eyes. Sitting on the garden fence at two in the morning, in the middle of a snowstorm, was a robin. A keen amateur ornithologist, Christine recognised its distinctive shape. In the soft glow of the street lamp, she could actually see the red breast. Extraordinary behaviour for any bird, let alone a robin. She had never heard of birds flying at night in the snow; it simply did not happen and she was astonished. Automatically Christine found herself saying, 'Hello, Mum.' Once more it appeared that this was a powerful symbol, a robin battling against all the odds to bring a message of comfort from a loved one.

183

From ancient times robins have been considered special birds. One legend has it that the robin took a thorn from the head of Jesus on the cross. Pricking his breast it turned red with blood and has remained so ever since. They have always been considered as messengers from the spirit world and today the many stories of robins appearing to bereaved people would seem to confirm this theory.

Tony looked out upon the garden and reflected on what an excellent gardener his father had been. He missed his father a great deal but working in the garden gave him a sense of encouragement and of his father approving. One day while digging in the garden Tony noticed a little robin hopping very close to him and showing no sign of fear. Even when Tony began to dig the movement did not scare the bird away. The whole time Tony worked in the garden the robin stayed close by. Weeks passed and Tony realised with amazement that every time he went into the garden to work the robin appeared. One day after Tony had been bending down planting bulbs he straightened up to find the robin sitting on the handle of his spade. The bird was so close to Tony he could hardly believe it. Tony's wife came outdoors and he told her about the robin and its visits. She too had noticed but had said nothing. It was at that moment they realised that this was Tony's father's way of communicating, it confirmed what Tony had been feeling — a sense that whenever he was in the garden his father was never far away.

Sally and her mother Mary were keen birdwatchers. The family would laugh and call them twitchers but they knew that the two were extremely keen on their chosen hobby. Frequently they would drive to other parts of the country to see a rare bird, perhaps one that visited the British Isles only rarely. Despite their knowledge of a vast array of birds, Mary loved the humble robin most of all. The cheeky call and bold ways endeared the bird to Mary and she was always as thrilled to see one as any other species. On the day of Mary's fiftieth birthday, Sally called at her mother's house to help her celebrate with all the family. It was a beautifully warm April day and they enjoyed coffee on the lawn, strolling out through the patio doors from the lounge to enjoy the morning. They then gathered inside, preparing to leave for a local hotel for a celebratory lunch. To the astonishment of the family, through the open door hopped a robin. The bird stood for several seconds staring directly at Mary. No one moved a muscle, not wanting to scare this lovely little bird. Mary was thrilled and Sally said as it hopped outside once more, 'It clearly wanted to wish you a happy birthday.'

Only a few short weeks after her birthday, Mary died. Sally and her family were devastated and could not imagine life without their lovely, lively mother. Life, as everyone says at such times, goes on and it was with disbelief that the family found the first anniversary of Mary's death approaching. Wishing to be together on such a sad day the family arrived at the family home. The garden was full of colour as Sally wistfully opened the patio doors, recalling how happy the day of her mother's last birthday had been.

Stunned, the family gazed on as through the patio doors hopped a little robin! The bird hopped boldly onto the carpet, staying motionless for a little while before leaving again through the open doors. Tears slid down Sally's face and she said, 'That could only be a message.' Sally's father said that during the past year the patio doors had been opened many times but no bird had ever been inside. Softly Sally said to herself, 'Thank you, God.'

Hilda reminded me for all the world of the character in the children's book Mrs Pepperpot. Her tiny frame and crab-apple cheeks made one smile and although her face was creased with age her eyes still twinkled. At the age of ninety-two she told me that she was 'ready to go' and had all the funeral arrangements organised, even down to the food the mourners would eat. She stood at only four feet ten inches tall and yet was strong in body and mind, having worked hard all her life and brought up her family alone after the early death of her husband. Here she was in the twilight of her years, as strong-minded and cheerful as ever, ready to fly to the next world, as she put it.

Eventually she began to grow weaker and was confined to bed for only a short time before she died in her sleep. The day of her funeral would have an atmosphere of celebrating her life rather than mourning. It was a cold, sunny November day when Hilda's tiny, flower-laden coffin was carried into the beautiful old church. The church was chilly and as the sun went behind the clouds, the mourners shivered a little. The vicar had known Hilda well and spoke of their long association and how cheerful and welcoming she had always been. It was a beautiful service which culminated with words from the vicar who said that he was sure that at that moment in time Hilda's soul was on its way to heaven. At precisely that moment the sun broke through the clouds and poured through the stained-glass window directly on to the little coffin. It directed its beam like a spotlight. From the depth of the flowers resting on the coffin, something stirred and a huge, beautiful moth flew directly up inside the ray of light. It was one of those symbolic moments that stay in the memory for ever.

Of all nature's symbols, clouds are arguably the most dramatic. They fill us with wonder at their constantly changing shapes, colours and beauty. Who as a child has not lain on the grass in the heat of a summer's day and watched the clouds? Images such as chariots and animals can be identified in the skyscape. Occasionally, the imagery is so clear and powerful that it can only be construed as a sign.

'How is cloud outlined? What hews it into a heap? Or spins it into a web? Cold is usually shapeless, I suppose, extending over large spaces equally or with gradual diminution: you cannot have in the open air, angels and wedges, and coils, and cliffs of cold. Yet the vapour stops suddenly sharp and steep as a rock or thrusts itself across the gates of heaven in the likeness of a brazen

bar, or braids itself in and out, and across and across,
like a tissue of tapestry, or falls into ripples like sand,
or into waving shreds and tongues, as fire. On what
anvils and wheels is the vapour pointed, twisted,
hammered, whirled, as the potter's clay? By what hands
is the incense of the sea built up into domes of marble?'

JOHN RUSKIN

One brilliant summer Sunday afternoon, Alison and her parents set out in the family car for a picnic. Wanting to take full advantage of the lovely weather they left early to travel to their favourite spot. This was the place called Cowbridge Common in South Wales. On arriving at the common, Alison's father stopped the car and as he climbed out said to his family, 'Quickly, look at the sky.' In the very centre of an otherwise clear blue sky was the cloud formation of an angel. It was huge and perfect in every detail, even to a pair of precisely shaped wings. It was an awesome sight and Alison and her parents stared in fascination. Soon the traffic started to build up as many motorists stopped their cars to stare at this amazing cloud angel. The common was filled with people gazing in wonderment at the sight. It remained so clear for such a long time that Alison says it is etched in her memory.

Unknown to Alison at the time, her mother was seriously ill. Her parents had thought to keep it from Alison as she was young and they wanted to spare her as much worry as possible. The kidney disease that Alison's mother suffered from claimed her life some months later. Alison came to the conclusion that the angel sign was to assure her that her mother would be taken care of by the angels, and she finds that thought and the memory of the cloud a huge comfort.

Our second cloud story involves a young lady being admitted to hospital for an operation. The operation was major surgery and although it was necessary there was also the element of fear as to what might be revealed. Louise climbed from the car, trying hard to control rising panic as her husband lifted the suitcase from the boot. Together they went through the procedures involved with admittance and finally they were shown to a small side ward. The room contained two beds but the other one, much to Louise's joy, was empty. It would be very hard to chat and be friendly, she thought, and wanted only to be alone. Her husband left, saying he would be back that evening at visiting time.

Routine tests were carried out and Louise was told that the operation would take place the following morning. The day went by very slowly; she tried to read but simply could not concentrate. The nurses were very kind and tried to help her relax but nothing seemed to make any difference. At one point the surgeon called in to the little room and although his calm confidence helped momentarily, the minute he left the panic rose once more. Visiting time saw her husband and friends chatting encouragingly and for a while she felt love and support boost her morale. It would be a difficult night, however, and she was sure that there would be little chance of sleep.

Waking early after a fitful night, Louise raised the blind in the little room and looked outside. It was a beautiful morning with the promise of a warm day ahead although it was still very early. Tearful, she did the only thing she could think of at that moment and that was to pray. Closing her eyes she asked God to help her on this very stressful occasion. After a moment or so meditating on this prayer she opened her eyes. The sight that met her gaze was breathtaking. There in the centre of an otherwise clear blue sky was a perfect cloud angel! It was very large and perfect in every detail, especially the wings, which seemed to spread above the cloud figure's head and reach below the edge of its long gown.

Tears fell again, but this time they were tears of gratitude. Louise knew that this was the answer to her prayer; there would be an angel watching over her that morning in the operating theatre. A deep sensation of peace filled her and she relaxed for the first time, convinced that all would be well. I am happy to report that indeed it was.

Ever since he could remember, John had worried about the protection of his home. This is not so surprising when one considers that he had in fact been the victim of burglary, with all the awful insecure feelings this crime leaves behind. He says that he also had a burning desire to see an angel: fascinated by these beings, he dearly wished for the comfort of knowing their protection. To his utter amazement, when he least expected it, protection from an angelic source appeared. John lives in a flat situated in the middle of a high-rise building. This building is the middle one of three. Many times he had to work away from home and always worried about security.

John's place of employment is actually only a five-minute walk from his home. From the top floor he can actually see the rear view of his block of flats. It was 6.25 pm on 10 July 2001 when John walked into an office at the top of the building. He was busy closing the windows before leaving for the day. Looking out he saw the most amazing sight. It was in fact a cloud, but one so astonishing it took his breath away. It was unmistakably an angel, its outline distinct, hands folded in prayer in front of its face, wings fully spread out behind and a long flowing gown. Most remarkable of all, this angel cloud was distinctly different from others in the distance. This cloud was dense and solid in appearance, whilst the others were white and faint by comparison. Remarkably, the background clouds moved swiftly in the sky, whilst the angel cloud remained stationary.

'I knew instantly what I was seeing,' says John, having often read about angels appearing in the guise of clouds. Here at last was John's special angel, hovering only a few feet above his own roof. He found himself spontaneously offering a prayer of gratitude and considers himself very blessed indeed.

I have to confess that my knowledge of ducks is virtually non-existent. Perhaps if pressed, I might identify a mallard on a park lake, but that would be the sum total of my expertise. The attraction they hold as a species for many people is easy to see but Joyce was so besotted by the duck family that she longed to own one as a pet. As long as she could remember, even as a child, she had longed to own a duck. The family had always kept dogs, which the children found much more fun, and she had to concede that dogs and ducks definitely should not mix. Joyce's one consolation was that their close neighbours actually kept ducks. She was welcome to see them whenever she wished and she loved to watch them waddle around the garden. The fluffy chicks were especially attractive to her and held a special place in her affections.

To the family's great distress, on 11 July 2000 Joyce died and was certain to be dreadfully missed. The following morning her daughter Janet heard the dog barking loudly and, rushing to see what the matter could be, she followed him into the garden. At the bottom of the garden was Joyce's own flower patch, where she had worked to make a special place for her to sit and read. The dog was agitated and barking at this particular area. Peering into the patch of flowers, Janet was taken aback at the sight of a duckling nestling in the very centre. At a loss, Janet went for their neighbour, who was an expert on the subject of ducks as well as keeping them.

The neighbour scratched his head, mystified at the sight of the duckling. 'Well,' he said at last, 'it is all very strange, firstly because this is a wild duck and certainly not one of mine. Secondly it is too tiny to fly so I cannot image how it arrived here. Thirdly there are no wild ducks anywhere near this area. The habitat is completely wrong – it is essential that ducks have rivers or ponds to sustain them and this area has neither.' No mother duck was found in the area even after an extensive search. To this day the duckling's arrival remains a mystery. Janet and her family could only ponder the symbolism of it all.

When leading a workshop one's hope is for a happy harmonious atmosphere, and above all for the ability to communicate. One wishes to be understood and indeed to understand. Gill was planning two workshops on the beautiful Welsh island of Anglesey. It felt highly appropriate to be holding them in a place of such natural beauty. Very much looking forward to the day, Gill prepared thoroughly and hoped that the workshop would hold an atmosphere of love and friendship. It would, she hoped, be a day of spiritual awareness.

The day began and almost from the very first minutes it became obvious to Gill that the warm atmosphere she had wanted was simply not in evidence. It can only get better, she thought; maybe as the day progresses things will improve. However, this was not to be and the whole day became a struggle. The key to any form of teaching is communication and wearily Gill said to her colleague, 'We are not getting through.' Late in the afternoon, there was a period of meditation. Each member of the group was asked to try to picture their own guardian angel. Silently Gill asked the angels for their help, beseeching them to show her a way of being understood. The meditation came to an end and people chatted in groups.

This being an area where Welsh is spoken, many ladies were conversing in Welsh. Anyone who has ever tried will tell you that Welsh is a very difficult language to learn. Most fluent speakers have been brought up with Welsh as their mother tongue. One lady talking in Welsh said to her friend that she felt most disappointed not to have seen her angel during meditation. Gill quickly replied that she must not worry, there were many other ways of contact, perhaps in a dream. It was only at this point that Gill realised she had understood every word the lady had said, even though she had no knowledge of the Welsh language! Just who was the most surprised it was difficult to say, but Gill's plea to the angels to allow her to communicate had been answered in a most amazing way.

Young people love to travel, the further the better it seems. England and Australia in particular seem to have a constant flow of young people between the two countries. Samia was no exception, a young Australian lady with itchy feet to see Europe. Soon she was living and working in London, making friends and enjoying life to the full. As the mother of one of Samia's new friends, Irene came to know and like Samia. She frequently visited Irene's home where the two formed a firm friendship after their initial instant rapport.

Six years passed and inevitably Samia found herself feeling very homesick from time to time. It was decided that she would go home for a long visit to her much loved and greatly missed family. Christmas was approaching and it would be a wonderful time to be back for the family festivities. Irene hugged her goodbye and wished her a safe trip, urging her to give her love to her nearest and dearest so far away. With great excitement Samia was waved off, longing to see home again after so many years.

Back in England, Christmas festivities were in full swing, with just two weeks to go before Christmas Day. Irene and her husband went to for a dinner dance, full of seasonal cheer. It was a lovely, elegant affair and Irene had looked forward to it immensely. The evening was a huge success and in the early hours they arrived home extremely tired but very happy. It was difficult to wake quickly when the telephone rang at 5 am. Lifting the phone in some confusion, Irene was surprised to hear the voice of Samia's mother calling from Australia. The phone call rocked Irene's happy world, for the dreadful news that morning was the fact that Samia had been killed in a car crash. It was almost impossible to take in the information and Irene wandered round all that day completely stunned. Samia felt like a daughter to her and she was devastated.

In England the time of the funeral found Irene and her husband and friends sitting together and playing Samia's favourite music. They meditated in an effort to join the mourners so far away. Samia was obviously a much loved and popular young lady as 350 of her friends attended the funeral. To celebrate her life and love of nature a ceremony was then arranged to scatter her ashes by the sea. There was a point on the headland where a beautiful lighthouse stood and it was here that the ashes were thrown out to sea. Beautiful frangipani flowers were tossed into the waves in a moving and beautiful gesture. Irene had a feeling down inside that one day she would visit this spot in Byron Bay to add her blessings and say goodbye properly to her lovely young friend.

Eventually the day arrived when Irene visited Australia. She rented a cottage by the sea from an agency in England and was astonished to find on arrival that it was called Frangipani Cottage. Already there was a link with the day of the funeral and the beautiful flowers thrown out to sea. This was Irene's personal goodbye as she walked onto the beautiful beach at Byron Bay accompanied by Samia's father. Carrying her wreath Irene walked to the water's edge. It was amazingly calm, like the proverbial Glass Sea; not a ripple could be seen. Samia's father said he had rarely seen the sea so calm at that point. Even more remarkable was the fact that they were alone on the beach, with not a soul in sight. True it was early morning, but usually there would have been people taking a morning swim. Saying some moving and private words Irene then threw her wreath into the water. The colour of the flowers against the blue sea and even bluer sky made a wonderful picture. Scarcely a ripple broke the surface and Irene felt a little sad that the flowers would simply sit almost at the water's edge. Minutes passed as they watched the beautiful flowers float motionless on the calm water. The stillness was very moving and after a little while Irene said, 'Goodbye, Samia,' and slowly the pair turned to go from the beach.

There followed the most extraordinary event. Suddenly from dead calm a single huge wave rushed up the beach and engulfed Irene and Samia's father. They found themselves waist-high in water, having only taken a couple of steps from its edge. Turning to face the sea again Irene felt a presence so strongly that she exclaimed, 'She is here!' She watched in awe as this single, huge wave retreated, having picked up the wreath and carried it out to sea. It was one of those spine-tingling moments never to be forgotten. The symbolism of the single wave, engulfing them seemingly in a wave of love has stayed with Irene to this day.

> *'Spirit of life, wind over flowing waters*
> *In earth, sea and sky,*
> *You are there.'*
>
> A PRAYER FROM IONA

Padma teaches yoga, Reiki and reflexology. It would be fair to say in fact that most days for Padma are spent giving treatments or lessons. Once a year, the groups of people practising yoga come together for a Christmas celebration. A buffet, a guest speaker on a seasonal topic and stalls with seasonal goods feature and the evening is much enjoyed by all. The Christmas of the year 2000 was to have an angel theme, a subject close to Padma's heart. Many healers believe their healing is angel-inspired and Padma is no exception. Arriving early at the hall to prepare for the evening, Padma was happy to see how spotless it was. Only tables and chairs to set into place before arranging her angel display and lighting candles to create a fitting atmosphere. It was a bitterly cold night but the hall was cosy, windows and doors firmly shut and very effective heating wafting the fragrance from the candles with a welcoming warmth.

Realising suddenly that she had forgotten the tape of music she intended to play, Padma announced to her helper that she would be gone for a moment. Hurrying home to pick up the music would take less than five minutes. Glancing around the room she was satisfied that all was ready, the empty tables at the end of the hall awaiting the display of angel crafts and books and the evening's fare. Her helper repaired to the kitchen to heat water for a welcoming drink for the people shortly to arrive on the cold winter night.

Rushing back, Padma was conscious on her return of a special atmosphere in the hall. Deciding it must be the fragrance and the angel statues, she plugged in the music to help the atmosphere even more. Turning to face the main body of the hall, she suddenly gasped. There under the tables where only moments ago there had been clean, clear floor was a pile of soft, white feathers! The doors and windows had remained locked and no one had entered the room. No wonder there was a special atmosphere. In the year 2000, Christmas, Ramadan and Chanukah all overlapped, a rare event in itself. The yoga party was held on the last night of Ramadan when it is believed that the angels are nearer the earth that at any other time during the year. What fitting symbolism the white feathers were.

Anyone who enjoys walking will be attracted to the Pennine Way. It is something of a Mecca for many people – wonderful scenery, peace and quiet and positive therapy for the soul. A keen walker, John would take to the hills whenever he felt the need for exercise and contemplation. The fresh air, occasional companionship of fellow walkers and the natural beauty were sufficient to charge his batteries once in a while. He was in a period of reflection after reading the Richard Bach book *Illusions*. Many people have found that his books give food for thought and John was no exception. He felt the need for a period in the fresh air and, packing his tent, set out to walk the Pennine Way.

From the very start this was no ordinary walk; many unusual sights and sounds reached John, nature seemed to have heightened colours and more symbolism than ever before. He met some remarkable people along the way and surprisingly the conversations were of a spiritual nature. The most unusual encounter was with a group of Buddhist monks. It was as if the deep spiritual feelings aroused by Richard Bach's books and the spiritual nature of the countryside were being constantly endorsed and confirmed by the conversations of everyone he met.

Walking alone one day after a night in his tent, John felt completely at one with nature and the world. It was the most beautiful clear day, deep blue skies and nature at the height of loveliness. He had been walking for some time, deep in thought, when suddenly he looked up to the sky. He found himself scarcely able to believe his eyes. There in the centre of an otherwise clear sky was a huge, white, cloud feather. Most cloud formations are, of course, horizontal. This feather was enormous and vertical, completely straight and perfect in every feature. Each frond of the feather was distinct and the tapering shape completely accurate. It was a breathtaking sight and quite unlike anything John had ever seen before. It felt like the ultimate message and symbolic of all his recent experiences. Fortunately John had his camera with him and the resulting photograph is quite stunning – in fact you will by now have realised that it is the one on the cover of this book.

> *'But what of the sheer beauty of the earth, that inspires love simply because it is so beautiful.'*
> IRENE HORNBY

$* *$ ✳ $* *$

Epilogue

Having researched the subjects of angel encounters and near-death phenomena for many years now, I have discovered one important fact above all others. I am convinced that I have merely scraped the tip of an angelic iceberg. For every generous and willing soul who is prepared to tell their story, several thousand keep their experiences private. Contact from the other world is far more common than anyone realises. Often people express the desire to have angels in their lives, asking how they might achieve it. The fact remains that we all have angels in our lives, it is just that they appear in forms not generally associated with angelic intervention. I have tried to illustrate in this book the fact that messages will arrive in the most unlikely of guises: unexpected, wonderful fragrances, bright lights, music, inanimate objects appearing at significant times, and the wonderful signs from nature. All are messages, and we receive what we can cope with. Not everyone needs a 'full blown' angel; we may simply require a sign.

Angels derive their name from the Greek *angelos*, meaning messenger. Their traditional role is that of intermediaries between the spiritual realm and Earth. Historically they have appeared more frequently in times of trouble, such as wars and dangerous epidemics, as in the Middle Ages when the population was ravaged by the plague. This was in fact the first time that art depicted angels as cherubs. Children were the first section of the community to succumb to the plague and every household would have mourned the death of a child. How comforting then to see paintings of cherubs and reflect on the thought that your own little one was an angel. The turn of the century also saw angels in large numbers reassuring people that all was well. A new millennium is almost always certain to raise fears for the future and therefore it is unsurprising to note that many more angel experiences were documented as we approached the year 2000.

The message delivered is always the same. You are not alone, love always surrounds you and guidance is there for the asking. Concentrate on the contents of your dreams, take notice of unusual fragrances, study the clouds and nature, your message could be waiting for you; try not to miss it. I shall leave you with the words of the great singer Pearl Bailey, who said, 'People see God every day; they just don't recognise him.'

✳ ✳ ✳ ✳ ✳

Further Reading

Anderson, Joan Wester, *Where Angels Walk* (Hodder & Stoughton, 1995)

Crosse, Joanna, *A Child's Book of Angels* (Barefoot Books, 2000)

Eadie, Betty J., *Embraced by the Light* (HarperCollins, 1995)

Fenwick, Dr Peter and Elizabeth, *The Truth in the Light* (Berkley Books, 1997)

Fontana, David, *The Secret Language of Symbols* (Duncan Baird, 2001)

Forder, John and Elizabeth, *The Light Within* (USHA Publications, 1995)

Heathcote-James, Emma, *Seeing Angels* (Blake Publishing, 2001)

Hope, Jane, *The Secret Language of the Soul* (Duncan Baird, 1999)

Linn, Denise, *Signposts* (Rider, 1999)

McLuhan, T.C., *The Message of Secret Places* (HarperCollins, 1997)

Moody, Raymond A., *Life After Life* (Rider, 2001)

Moolenburgh, H.C., *A Handbook of Angels* (The C W Daniel Company, 1984)

Morse, Dr Melvin, *Transformed by the Light* (Piatkus, 1993)

Rawlings, Dr Maurice, *Beyond Death's Door* (Bantam, 1991)

Rhodes, Leon, *Tunnel to Eternity* (Swedenborg Foundation, 1997)

Skafte, Diane, *Listening to the Oracle* (Harper SanFrancisco, 1997)

Wake, Wilma, *Crystals, Crosses and Chakras* (Chrysalis, 2000)

✴

Further Information and Resources

Near Death and Other Worlds Association
82 Ridgway Crescent
Orpington
Kent BR6 9QP
www.ndowa.com

Zodiac Zones
(Angel crafts, gifts, books, jewellery)
PO Box 7007
Hook
Hants RG27 8JP
Tel. 01252 843265

The Angel Connection
White Stone House
Grange Paddock
Mark
Somerset TA9 4RW

ANGEL
(Books, gifts, crystals)
PO Box 344
Manchester M60 2EZ

Cottage Crafts
(Paintings, pottery)
"Wincott"
2 Main Street
Sedgeberrow
Evesham
Worcestershire WR1 1BU

Jaimie Cahill
(Spiritually inspired artist)
Gallery
1 Cardwell Crescent
Oxford OX3 7QE

Brian Carter
(Music)
Walkinginharmony@ukonline.co.uk

AN ANGEL AT MY SHOULDER
True stories of Angelic Experiences
Glennyce S. Eckersley

An Angel at My Shoulder shows angels are returning – and being acknowledged – once again. Here are true stories of countless ordinary people being rescued by angels, being comforted and healed by them, feeling their presence in the face of death – and of angels often appearing to little children. These tales are drawn from such countries as Britain, Australia, Ireland and the United States – showing how angels can be found all round the globe: helping others, often changing their lives completely.

Warm and uplifting, *An Angel at My Shoulder* suggests it is more than time to reconsider our view of angels, to let them back into our hectic, mechanised world and to realise we are never alone . . .

'If you believe in angels Glennyce S. Eckersley's extraordinary true stories about angelic encounters will affirm your belief that angels are truly watching over us. If you don't believe in angels, you may find your non-belief wavering . . . This book touches the soul and opens the doors to the realm where heaven and earth meet and love abounds.'

DENISE LINN, author of *Sacred Space*

OUT OF THE BLUE
Modern-Day Miracles & Extraordinary Coincidences
Glennyce S. Eckersley

This book is about coincidences and modern-day miracles: the seemingly random acts that may well turn out to be not so random after all. How do they happen? — why? — and to whom?

Only in recent times have we felt alone and isolated in our universe. Yet for centuries men and women fervently believed in the intervention of a higher power in their lives. Today, as more of us search for greater spiritual fulfilment, we wonder once again whether such events might mean we live, not in a purely chaotic world, but rather in one of harmony, meaning and order at a deeper level.

Glennyce S. Eckersley has here collected many extra-ordinary true stories of coincidences in the everyday, in nature and in dreams — as well as spiritual stories and contemporary miracles from around the world. All of these suggest the many different things that happen to us must be fundamentally interconnected and meaningful — though they so often appear straight *out of the blue*.

If you would like to order any of the following or to receive our catalogue please fill in the form below:

An Angel at My Shoulder by Glennyce S. Eckersley	£6.99
Out of the Blue by Glennyce S. Eckersley	£6.99
Children and Angels by Glennyce S. Eckersley	£6.99
Angels and Miracles by Glennyce S. Eckersley	£6.99
May the Angels Be With You by Gary Quinn	£6.99
Heaven and Earth by James van Praagh	£8.99
Proud Spirit by Rosemary Altea	£6.99
Sacred Space by Denise Linn	£12.99

ALL VERMILION BOOKS ARE AVAILABLE THROUGH MAIL ORDER OR FROM YOUR LOCAL BOOKSHOP.

PAYMENT MAY BE MADE USING ACCESS, VISA, MASTERCARD, DINERS CLUB, SWITCH AND AMEX, OR CHEQUE, EUROCHEQUE AND POSTAL ORDER (STERLING ONLY).

EXPIRY DATE .... SWITCH ISSUE NO.

SIGNATURE ....

PLEASE ALLOW £2.50 FOR POST AND PACKING FOR THE FIRST BOOK AND £1.00 PER BOOK THEREAFTER.

ORDER TOTAL: £...............................(INCLUDING P&P)

ALL ORDERS TO:

VERMILION BOOKS, BOOKS BY POST, TBS LIMITED, THE BOOK SERVICE, COLCHESTER ROAD, FRATING GREEN, COLCHESTER, ESSEX CO7 7DW

TELEPHONE: (01206) 256 000
FAX: (01206) 255 914

NAME ....

ADDRESS ....

....

Please allow 28 days for delivery. Please tick box if you do not wish to receive any additional information ☐

Prices and availability subject to change without notice.